Leadership

Powerful Lessons in Personal Change

(How to Use Self Control and Mental Toughness to Achieve Your Goals)

Keith Gallegos

I0089868

Published By **Darby Connor**

Keith Gallegos

All Rights Reserved

*Leadership: Powerful Lessons in Personal Change
(How to Use Self Control and Mental Toughness to
Achieve Your Goals)*

ISBN   978-1-7775767-6-9

No part of this guidebook shall be reproduced in any form without permission in writing from the publisher except in the case of brief quotations embodied in critical articles or reviews.

Legal & Disclaimer

The information contained in this book is not designed to replace or take the place of any form of medicine or professional medical advice. The information in this book has been provided for educational & entertainment purposes only.

The information contained in this book has been compiled from sources deemed reliable, and it is accurate to the best of the Author's knowledge; however, the Author cannot guarantee its accuracy and validity and cannot be held liable for any errors or omissions. Changes are periodically made to this book. You must consult your doctor or get professional medical advice before using any of the suggested remedies, techniques, or information in this book.

Upon using the information contained in this book, you agree to hold harmless the Author from and against any damages, costs, and expenses, including any legal fees potentially resulting from the application of any of the information provided by this guide. This disclaimer applies to any damages or injury caused by the use and application, whether directly or indirectly, of any advice or information presented, whether for breach of contract, tort, negligence, personal injury, criminal intent, or under any other cause of action.

You agree to accept all risks of using the information presented inside this book. You need to consult a professional medical practitioner in order to ensure you are both able and healthy enough to participate in this program.

Table Of Contents

Chapter 1: Leading Like Wolves

Wolves possess a stunning look. They look confident, calm and exude their "Don't mess with me" attitude. Since predators are a part of the pack, it's essential for wolves to exhibit these characteristics because they will make them more successful as a group.

Consider the wolf pack in terms of one group:

The team leader could be described as an alpha male in a wolf pack.

Team members have a commonality with other members of the group.

There's a shared dependency between the members of the pack as well as the male alpha. The survival of the pack is contingent on three factors:

1. The capacity of an alpha to determine the direction and goal. A confident and steadfast presence an alpha leader who can recognize

the opportunity to lead his team in its search for.

2. The abilities and synergies of the pack. Each Wolf in the pack needs to perform at their top performance in the hunt.

3. There is a trust factor between the crowd and the Alpha - Without this aspect, you have very little chance of being successful.

Setting the Direction

In terms of leadership From a leadership perspective, the alpha wolf picks the animal to hunt, but doesn't chase it on its own. If the prey was tiny, pursuing it on its own might be possible, however generally the wolves would rather hunt larger prey, which demands that the entire group.

The Alpha identifies an opportunity and recruits his group to help. The method is typically consistent: seek out the most young most vulnerable, weakest, oldest or the most easily accessible targets as means to ensure the effort only goes to accomplish a goal.

The same applies to the leadership who are in charge of establishing an overall strategy and vision or pursuing new market opportunities which could lead to revenue growth for the business. They will not achieve their goals without the team of skilled employees.

Skills and Synergy

The pack members are assigned specific roles when hunting. There are some who prefer to be engaged in the action, while some might be more in an advisory role, and remain in the background. But, every role plays a crucial role in building and maintaining the fitness and stage of the group.

This is also true for organizations. Every employee has an important contribution to the achievement of the organization regardless of where they are within the "chain of command". It's the duty for the top executives in the organization to make sure that every employee is aware in order to increase employee satisfaction and retain them.

Mutual Trust and Respect

There's a distinct hierarchy among wolf packs. There is an Alpha on highest of pole and an omega on the bottom. Within the team structure, there's still a sense of every wolf's importance and role. Every wolf is a key part in their "society".

Leaders must be able within the company to appreciate the teams and individuals that aid them in reaching their goals. Invaluing them as a commodity and shaming them by imposing bad work conditions undermines confidence and trust.

An insufficiency in Wolf Leadership's strategy. Wolf Leadership strategy

In the past, I've identified a handful of things which make good leaders of wolves. However, there is a crucial point to remember. A typical success rate for hunting wolves is thought to range from three to 15 percent. This is a very low number! In all the great qualities they've got going on for them, you'd think they would have more success, right?

According to several studies, this issue could be due to their inability to coordinate and communications. This is quite surprising, isn't it?

This is a problem we see across organizations, too. The communication within the company is essential. Insufficient communication at all levels leads to projects being ruined and a lot of unnecessary work or projects that are discarded. Communication is something that we have be aware of for us to work more effectively and boost the chances of succeeding.

In conclusion, take an examination of the table below that examines the traits of leadership needed by the leader of an organization and an alpha Wolf.

Organizational Leadership. Alpha Wolf

Trait Organizational Leader Alpha Wolf

Direction Plans vision and objectives and organizes teams to bring these goals a reality. Defines what the objective is and guides the team in pursuit of the target

Synergy is dependent on the team as well as their leaders working toward the desired goals. Leverages all the advantages of the team to increase the chances of successful outcomes

Respect and Mutual Trust and Respect The need to build trust and empower the team members in the field so that they can maximize their talents. allows the remainder of the group to apply their talents and win collectively

In the next chapter we review of a predator which is known to have a greater success percentage... that of the Cheetah.

Chapter 2: Leading Like Cheetahs

My child was in kindergarten when he was in kindergarten, he took home artwork depicting the cheetah. The caption that was included is "The cheetah is my favorite animal because it can run very fast." Oh what a sweet innocence five-year-old!

Everyone knows that the cheetah has the distinction of being the quickest animal that lives on earth. It is among the most obvious advantages. However, this alone isn't what makes the cheetah a successful animal. The cheetah must take a very calculated approach to how to use this ability. You must consider:

Which situations call for speed? The speed of a car isn't the answer to every problem.

How and when you can use speed. It could be only component of a solution. Most often, it has to be used in conjunction with increased perception, stealth, or the use of camouflage.

The limits of speed. A Cheetah is not able to maintain its maximum speed forever. The acceleration aspect must be carefully planned.

In the case of animals like the cheetah the decisions they make are intuitive by the fact that they are member of nature. As humans are, we need more consideration about the optimal utilization of our talents.

Understanding when, where and how to apply your strengths

There are many steps to follow in a hunt for cheetahs that include stalking, detection and approach, chase and then capture. From all of these, the one that needs quickness is "chase". Thus, speed must be maintained for the duration of hunting. This is the way cheetahs think of thinking about strategies.

The leaders of an organization have to be able to strategize about the choices they take regarding their organization. A simple choice at the same time during the year can cause disastrous consequences at another time. In particular, retail stores must make specific arrangements for peak seasons like holiday seasons like Christmas and Thanksgiving. It is important to note that plans to increase capacity with regards to people processes, technology and people can only be sustained for a brief period. In the long run, maintaining this level over the course of the year could hurt the overall morale of the organization and employees.

Retail leaders are given the possibility of strategizing on the best way to smooth shifts between peak seasons and throughout the year, other executives are similarly able to plan regarding processes that are specific to their particular industry or company. Leaders who are truly successful have the capability in coming up with fresh ways to become more effective.

Understanding the limitations of your strengths

The cheetah is aware that it is able to run only at the speed of light for short periods of time. This is the reason it runs close to the prey, before running after it and then pimping at the animal. It realizes the significance in preserving its power to ensure its effectiveness.

Similar to this, we should look at an organization's products distribution strategy. The use of a single channel, for example, brick and mortar retailer could limit their revenue stream, and place a strain on their channel. Dependence on one channel can lead to a lack of efficiency and, ultimately, the reduction in sales. Companies must accommodate different channels, including mobile as well as online sales i.e. online sales in order to grow the number of customers they serve and their revenue.

Learn from the success of the cheetah's rate

Cheetah's hunting success rate is believed to be at least fifty percent. It's quite remarkable when contrasted with the wolf's level of successful hunts. It is due to the cheetah's abilities and strategy. Because the cheetah generally is an individual hunter, they do not require communications and coordination issues that are required in a pack of wolves.

In a way one could think about the way companies structure themselves. Flat-shaped companies, i.e. having less hierarchy, tend to have lower levels of management and are generally more effective than those that have more of a higher-level hierarchy. Teams have more autonomy and have less administrative restrictions they can accomplish their tasks. Teams are more flexible and are more likely to manage themselves.

For a summary, have note of the chart below, which compares the characteristics of leadership required by an organizational leader as well as the cheetah.

Organizational Leader Vs. Cheetah

Strength Factors Organizational Leader Cheetah

Strategy Recognize that a single approach isn't appropriate for to all situations. Strategies for optimal utilization of speed

There are limitations when using Multiple Distribution Channels as opposed to a single channel in order to maximize the growth. Know that speed alone won't bring the success you desire. Other abilities like the ability to track and stealth are also vital.

Chapter 3: Leading Like Giraffes

In the chapters before we have looked at the species that are thought to be predators within the natural world. However, predators aren't the only ones in the animals' world.

Let's consider the giraffes for instance. They are the plant eaters. Giraffes prove that it is not necessary to be aggressive to become an effective leader. Their methods and skills could differ from those of predators, but their skills are beneficial to them and their youngsters keep safe. The three main traits which give giraffes a competitive advantage are camouflage, height as well as strength.

These characteristics are utilized as they attempt to gain an advantage over prey:

The giraffes sense danger at an early stage and alert other Giraffes by leveraging their height for increased surveillance.

Learn to recognize and guard yourself from risks that could be posed by using their camouflage when they are in the imminent threat.

Be brave and face challenges with confidence using their strength and power to fight predators should they come close.

Strength comes from numbers Forging coalitions to safeguard their children.

This is a major role in the survival of animals in the natural. These same characteristics can be used in an organization setting.

Vigilance and Risk Assessment

Giraffes' height, combined with its keen eyesight, lets it see threats from a distance. It allows for a herd of giraffes to respond and safeguard themselves at any time. They have to be able to make quick decisions being able to determine if animals within close proximity pose dangers, and alert the herd in a timely manner.

In the same way, it's the job of any leader of any business to ensure the wellbeing of employees and the business. Leaders must take sound decisions beneficial to the entire organization. It is essential to be aware of trends in the market or the industry, and then decide the best course of action to take for the company.

The choices made should be evaluated in relation to the risks and possible consequences on the business. Certain decisions could be higher risk. But when the rewards overshadow the risks and the potential impact, then an executive might consider worthwhile.

Courage

Giraffes aren't predators, however they are able to stop them. The strong hind legs of giraffes are frequently employed to strike powerful punches at predators. They do this in order in order to defend themselves and their offspring.

Any leader within an organization must be a strong leader. They should be able to defend their choices and be a strong advocate for their teams as well as provide the direction and belief for the employees of the company. These are all things that require confidence. Refraining from or being hesitant to "ruffling a few feathers" is a sign of a weak leader.

The act of bringing a group together (for the sake of a common goal)

Giraffes are believed to belong to a "Fission-Fusion" society. They function in a way that is independent from one another, yet may come together in times of need. They typically form a coalition of nursery mothers in order to look after their children with one another. Although this is a good protection, it's believed that less than twenty percent of giraffes who are young reach adulthood. They are particularly targeted by young giraffes since they lack energy and endurance.

For an organisation that is a part of an organization, it's the job of the manager to put individuals who are suitable to accomplish a specific goal. It is a matter of identifying those who have the right capabilities and skills, as well as the ones who would be suited to the job. It is the responsibility of coordination and bringing everyone together to achieve the same goal is on the person in charge. They also have to determine the strengths of their team as well as the gaps in their skills and the best way to deal with these.

External factors that are beyond the control of the giraffe

Giraffes are also subject to factors that could threaten their lives. The main reason for this is caused by human intervention as well as encroachment. The result is decreasing the size of the giraffe's population. The issue is being tackled by bringing awareness to this issue and the involvement conservation groups in order to alleviate and correct the issue.

Leaders of organizations also face uncertainties and risk. They must often plan for the unknown by creating an action plan to mitigate the risk. Sometimes, this means outsourcing specific tasks to reduce or shift the risks to the company.

For a summary, have an examination of the table below that compares the traits of leadership required by an organizational leader as well as an one-of-a-kind giraffe.

Organizational leader vs. Giraffe

Strength Factors Organizational Leader Giraffe

Be aware of markets and market conditions, and making any adjustments or changes required. Uses his height and eyesight to spot potential dangers early and notify to the herd.

Courage has a confident and assured approach to solving problems The brave face of Courage stands firm against predators and put up the fight when necessary

Gain Alignment brings together people who have the skills required to move toward a common objective. together to accomplish specific goals e.g. caring for children

Chapter 4: Assess Your Comfort Level

Have you ever considered that animals might provide us with information on how to become more effective leader?

In the earlier sections, we discussed several of the traits of leadership demonstrated by the wolf the giraffe, and cheetah and the ways we can implement these characteristics in our company. We will look at some of the characteristics that a great leader should have.

Making decisions (and telling "No")

Leadership involves making decisions. If leaders use an algorithm for making decisions based on data however, they might be forced to take decisions that do not go well by their colleagues or teams, e.g. in cases where their decision-making process is contrary to the opinion of their team. The consensus can be beneficial when it is needed, but leaders should not just wait until consensus is reached in order to propel their work ahead.

The leader shouldn't fixate about being liked by everyone. It's impossible to get everyone's approval. As humans, we strive to do our best the way we treat ourselves and those around us. In the same way, businesses and their managers strive to do their best for their employees, the company and customers. In the process you will encounter those who don't align with your objectives which is why you should accept without being a victim.

Both vertically and horizontally (with others and with leaders)

As an administrator, you'll be required to provide directions or details to your colleagues as well as your bosses. This will require confidence and ability to communicate. It is essential to recognize that the number of specifics can differ for each class.

Vertical communication with the executives and supervisors demands an eloquent and precise message that they are able to use to analyze the business's performance and take the appropriate decisions.

In horizontal presentations to your peers On the other hand needs more details. The reason is that peers require this information in order to help the team and you.

Delegation

It is an educational institution, home and company, it's generally impossible for one person to be able to manage all of the tasks. In the event that the tasks involved in one of these organizations is very small There must be separation of duties. In the absence of this, there could be burning out and overwork.

Leaders must feel comfortable giving up controlling and transferring work to other people by establishing specific expectations for the outcomes. This enables the leader to concentrate on strategic issues as well as develop higher performers in teams and individuals.

An experienced leader will not think of delegation as a threat rather, a way to provide the people with more opportunities to be leaders and develop. This helps build trust and loyalty and can help retain top the best talent.

Relying on the experts

They are not experts in all areas, however they should know the basics of their industry and business. For gaining knowledge about certain topics they must speak with experts and use their knowledge when needed. It's not wise to position a leader as an expert in the field even though there are other experts with an extensive amount of knowledge regarding the subject. People who are aware of what to do and when to use their own experts in-house do not think of them as potential threats to their authority as leaders. They instead take satisfaction in the knowledge that their company has the appropriate expertise to achieve its objectives.

Crediting other people

When you see a successful project and you are praised by your team for producing this positive result? Do you think your leadership is the primary factor in the success of your team? The majority of times it is a mix of both. The best leaders don't rely by their leadership skills and inspire, but instead, they thrive they are based on the accomplishments of their team. The leader should inspire the best qualities in team members and keep team spirits high.

The leaders who struggle to provide their teams credit generally feel insecure about their capacity to manage. They are worried that the team could be perceived as independent and diminish the value of the leader in the company. It isn't something that an authentic leader is worried with. The most effective leaders always keep an eye on the team's accomplishment and the credit when due.

Owning your mistakes

Did you have the pleasure of working with an executive who could refuse to admit that they had been incorrect? This could play out in several methods:

They place their team's in the dirt for making poor decisions

They defend their choice in spite of all the evidence that is in opposition to it

They're unable to acknowledge that they could have made better choices.

The kind of conduct that is exhibited does not benefit the leader, team and the business!

I've had the privilege of working with several leaders who have this issue and it's just irritating. As a leader myself I've observed that admitting an error and looking at the things that could be improved for the next time has allowed me to become a better and a trusted leader. As as a leader, I'm not there to make it appear like I have all the answers and will never make a mistake. It's pretentious and unreal. This would prevent my team, colleagues and my superiors from seeing me in my full potential as an effective leader.

Leadership Survey

It is worth taking your time to examine the above mentioned factors and determine the place where you're comfort is with every one of them. Make use of a scale that is listed below for each of the factors to identify your current leadership level. This will allow you to easily determine if you're ready to lead, or the behaviors you'll should tweak (or for which ones to get instruction for) in order to be a better leader.

How do I begin?

In order to become a more effective leader, it is essential to start by focusing on your own self. Making the most of your mental attitude and character is the very first step in succeeding. It is all about bringing the best out of individuals. It means that the leader, need to concentrate on ways to enable others to thrive and achieve the best success overall.

There are numerous opportunities outside of organizations where leaders can take on leadership. In the next chapters, we will explore these possibilities by presenting examples of leaders at work.

Chapter 5: At Work

Every workplace regardless of whether business, startup small business or non-profit, needs the leadership of a person to succeed

Leaders' primary responsibilities within this context include:

1. Define the vision, mission and mission of the business

Establish expectations about the way of life

Choose the individuals needed for the achievement of the vision.

Assist individuals in becoming leaders for themselves.

Share ideas for improving the efficiency of operations

While the two first points mentioned above could be performed by an executive leader or the founder of an organization however, the remaining work can be completed any person regardless of the rank or position.

Let's examine Anya who is a leader in her workplace as well as how she does on taking the Leadership survey.

Being a Leader at Work

Anya is Director of Innovation within a tiny insurance firm. She supervises several teams, and is accountable to the Chief Operating Officer. In her role as Director of Innovation she is expected to gather information and develop suggestions about the development of the company and its ability to compete. This requires working with an array of employees both inside as well as outside of the business.

Making decisions (and Saying "No")

They are typically responsible for making the final decision for their department, team or company. Anya certainly cannot take the decision on her own. She must consult inside experts as well as professionals from the industry before arriving at the final conclusion on particular concepts. The decisions she makes aren't always made in a consensus. It is important to feel at ease with rescinding concepts that are not in line with the company's overall plan or are a risk to the financials or elsewhere. Anya will also make sure that if she decides to turn off ideas, she supports her decisions with evidence and logic. It helps others consider her reliable and trustworthy.

Both vertically and horizontally (with colleagues and leaders)

If you're an individual leader or leader, you'll always be working with colleagues, team members and managers. Anya also has to work cross-organizationally to complete her innovation initiatives. It is her responsibility to go through some initial thoughts for innovations by her manager to gain an organizational perspective of alignment as well as assess the team she'll need and then instruct teams to take what they should do next. In the event that there are dependencies with multi-functional teams, she needs communicate with her colleagues in order to verify that the timelines of their teams are in line with hers.

Delegation

When Anya receives the team approvals and the teams are established, her role will be more of a servant leader starting from then on. That is, she is expected to help and guide the team when they face difficulties of any kind. In other words, she must be able to trust that the team will complete the work. Being able to consistently being informed of the work of the team allows her to keep an ear on the pulse of the team, without having to micromanage the team.

Conferring to experts

While Anya manages the business policy around innovations, she requires the support of tech and business experts in order to develop a well-thought-out strategy. Their insights and suggestions from the experts will help her assess the viability of a plan or provide her an understanding of the risks associated with every idea.

Giving credit to other people

To be a good manager, Anya makes it one of her most important goals for teams to be encouraged to develop innovative ideas. Inspiring team members to be in charge of their own work will allow teams to develop ways to change existing practices, either through a procedure or technological perspective.

Anya Always makes it her goal to attribute credit to the person who came up with the idea. This does not just encourage more innovative concepts, but can also make people feel that they're in the right place to influence change.

Owning your mistakes

In order to be successful in the field that is "Innovation", it is essential to be a person of experimentation i.e. take a risk, test the outcomes, then refine and re-do the task until you are satisfied with the result is reached. Anya is always committed to never being scared to fail because she believes that each failure can provide an abundance of valuable knowledge that can be used to inform another iteration of the concept's execution.

In the event that an idea fails to bring the expected outcomes, Anya takes ownership of this situation in order to provide all the information needed to the leaders as well as her coworkers. Because she oversees teams as well, she's also responsible for the performance of the teams she supervises. She has the responsibility of describing the reasons why an idea failed and then the actions taken to improve an idea in order to get the desired results.

Chapter 6: In The Community

Communities may be founded upon the place of residency and ethnic origins, as well as interests or any other reason that binds people because of common experiences or just because of the values they hold.

In order for communities to succeed They require individuals who can guide the actions of their community to a vision that is shared.

The leaders of the community generally have the following qualities:

Bring people closer

Build connections beyond the boundaries of your community.

Create a direction and set standards for the entire community.

Recognize and respond to the demands of the people in your community.

They must lead in influencing, influence, bargaining and also communicate, while remaining conscious of the voices of the people in their communities.

Being a Leader in the Community

Misha is an active member in her church. Her responsibilities include leading meetings concerning plans for community gatherings fundraising, special prayer and fund-raising. It is an enjoyable task as well as her organizational and communication capabilities help her to execute plans flawlessly.

Making Choices (and Saying "No")

In any society There are many perspectives as well as opinions and ideas which cannot be always accepted. Misha is required to reconcile her temple's needs alongside ideas and suggestions from the greater group of people. While all the ideas in her group are well-intentioned but not every one can be put into practice. Misha must carefully review these ideas in conjunction with the other community leaders to weigh the total impact before deciding whether to go forward with the idea or not. Misha must also ensure that those who have ideas which aren't picked, are kept up-to-date and invited to contribute in implementation of some of the chosen suggestions. This is how Misha acknowledges the leadership in the community she lives in.

Both vertically and horizontally (with colleagues and leaders)

Misha needs to get approval from the city or even from the temple board in the case of certain events she's in charge of. Then she recruits volunteers to bring the event to life. It is important for her to become viewed as likable and likable, while also being as a leader within the eyes of temple officials and other organisations with which they collaborate.

Delegation

As energetic as Misha can be, she is unable to manage events or create events within the temple without the support of volunteers and other individuals with the necessary abilities.

They must be able to trust them who are trustworthy and accountable and usually checks their character through establishing a rapport with them, allowing her to know their talents, passions as well as their versatility. Matching them to the best work can yield better results.

Relying on the experts

After establishing connections, Misha understood who could assist her in specific projects. As an example, certain people are adept at managing food services while others excel at performing cultural shows, and some specifically know the components necessary for particular religious celebrations. The group is able for help in executing particular tasks or seek their opinion on what's required to get all the required resources.

Giving credit to other people

A community can't exist with its people. It's the interaction of members that help the community to create the desired positive impact on its members.

Misha is committed to giving awards and recognition to all those who contribute to making an event or change take place in the temple. This improves the overall health of the congregation as a overall and helps keep people engaged.

Chapter 7: At Home

In order for a house to function effectively, it must have an element of order. Without it, there'd only confusion, chaos and anxiety.

The home may have various combinations. Here are a few instances:

Children and parents

Grandparents, parents, and children

A couple

A Bachelor/Bachelorette

In every one of these situations each of these scenarios, there's a need to be a leader. The following example further explores the demands and challenges of being a good leader in the home.

Being a Leader at Home

Jay as well as Maya are parents to an teen and a teenager. According to their experiences they have found that each phase require a great deal of patience, tact and some assertiveness. As with all executives, leaders must be able to demonstrate some of the qualities or characteristics described in the earlier section, such as taking decisions, delegating and embracing the mistakes they make, and so on.

Let's examine how each of these traits can be applied to Jay and Maya's journey to leadership in their home.

Making decisions (and Refusing to say "No")

The teenage and tween years may be difficult to get through. The time when kids begin becoming more self-sufficient and swayed. As parents, we ought to encourage such behaviors as it will make them more successful in the end time. We must, however, take a close look at situations, and also be able to say "No" and be ready to confront the commotion or music which follows.

Then, one day, their teenage thought he didn't have to study for his exams, and wanted to just spend time with his friends and watching films instead. This indicated the parents Jay and Maya required to step in and provide direction. They realized that they may get a rude response or silence, or even a know-it-all approach, but this is normal given the heightened hormones of teens. Jay and Maya were able to avoid taking this as a personal attack, instead set up a plan for the boy e.g. "Spend X hours studying before you watch TV or spend time with your friends." They would also lay security rails that would help him keep his focus.

It is true that teens are still growing physical as well as emotionally. The fact that this is the case is supported by numerous scientific studies on the brain of teenagers. The limbic system that regulates behavior that is impulsive or risky, is much more developed than the frontal lobe which is the brain's control center for solving problems and making decisions. This results in greater risk-taking and reckless decisions.

Parents such as Jay and Maya must put on an empathetic face and collaborate with teens and tweens in order to resolve issues or make them do specific chores.

Both vertically and horizontally (with others and with leaders)

Parents must ensure that they're in the same place with regards to decision making. Children can discern differences in their parents' viewpoints and utilize this information to benefit themselves. This is something I know through personal experiences!

Jay and Maya take slightly different approaches in parenting. Maya frequently finds herself as "Bad Cop". She is forced to actively communicate with Jay and make sure they show one unit to the children. Maya realizes that communication is crucial with transparency, honesty and establishing expectations.

When Maya agrees with Jay regarding the directions for the children, she will relay her ideas to children. As each parent is in the same boat so that the children can't detect any loopholes. Maya makes sure she does not speak to children in a smug way. A tone like this will just make children more resistant to her suggestions.

Delegation

Mothers such as Maya tend to make the mistake of believing that they have to manage all things. It is often due to an urge to stay at the helm. This isn't always a good thing however it should be balanced by allowing people to grow and learn.

A particular job Maya has a particular zeal about is loading dishwashers. She's very specific about what to do with the bowls and plates in order that there are more dishes within a single dish. The majority of the time, she wants to handle this chore by herself.

What Maya must force herself to do is clearly convey her worries or show better methods to load the dishwasher. If she is a coach and is willing to help her children learn essential life skills in addition to having people to assist her with the job and also focus on other essential household chores or work tasks.

Conferring to experts

We as parents think that we're experts on everything, especially when it comes with our kids, don't we? But, there are instances where it is necessary communicate with our spouses, educators financial advisors or homeowners' advisors in order for help with issues regarding our finances, homes or children.

Jay and Maya may, for instance, seek financial advice from advisors in order to take care of their financials and investments for a secure future for their families.

Giving credit to other people

Couples will always have distinct skills. That's what makes the perfect group. As a group deserves recognition when they have done well, the couples should acknowledge each other as well as their children whenever they think of concepts or resolve problems in the household.

Jay and Maya are in a good relationship, and they show their appreciation to each other as well as towards their children. Jay and Maya specifically take the time to acknowledge the teachers who help their kids persevere and excel with activities such as sport and music.

Participation of parents is essential however, their friends or partners shape their children's experiences in order so that they can be more balanced. Crediting the teachers suggests that parents are confident with their job as well as very confident as they play a supporting part of certain tasks.

Owning your mistakes

As as a parent, I strive to remain calm, however this isn't always feasible. Particularly when there's no co-operation from my children and/or my husband. These situations cause me to often lose my sanity. Then, it's usually and is followed by a sense of regret.

Jay and Maya are faced with conflicts and problems sometimes. These issues vary from as easy like who gets to carry garbage out, to choosing the best schools or activities that their children should be involved in. The stress of their jobs can make their tolerant, and they don't have control over their moods.

Recovery for them both is admitting that they've had a bad relationship with one another or their children and to explain their position to ensure that those in the other party's position will understand that it's not meant to be interpreted as a personal attack. Also, they reflect on ways they might better deal with similar situations in the future.

Chapter 8: At School

As a parent of children who have been around throughout their elementary and high school years and beyond, I am able to say that children begin to realize their potential to be leaders in the early years of the age of elementary school. It can take the forme of being "bossy", but at the age of 10 the word "bossy" can be seen as a sign of confidence enough to lead.

A few kids seem to be active in the elementary and middle school. They then begin to discover their voices in high school. The way they lead in high school is distinct from the one you see in the classroom. Students in high school cannot be able to get away by having the status of "bossy" due to push away from classmates. The leaders here are more proactive and have a knack for taking responsibility and delegating to the group of others.

There are many opportunities to be a leaders at all levels of the school. Below are some of the opportunities:

Elementary School - Group contests and activities require the individuals who coordinate, split and finish the task.

Middle School students have the opportunity to be mentors for children at elementary school. In addition, coordinating the student club as well as participating in national competitions encourages leadership among these students.

High School Sports captains as well as band section leader and club leaders are instances of roles that students have the opportunity to practice and develop their leadership abilities. Sometimes, they end up becoming role models, or even their primary source of information for colleagues.

We will look at the role of a leader in the middle school age group in relation to Leadership survey.

Being a Leader at School

Sam is in seventh grade. Sam is an extremely hardworking student who is a part of the Yearbook club as well as the Cross-country team of the school. He's very social and always seeking for ways to involve people in the activities offered by the school. He is loved by teachers and his fellow students.

Making Choices (and Saying "No")

Being an integral participant in the yearbook group, Sam has to ensure that the members participate in the activities. He must be aware of those in charge of the organization needs help in coordinating and managing the activities.

There are times when, even in an organisation with 10 to 20 members, there are bound to have a variety of opinion. In the case of initiatives Sam is the one on the hook, he needs to feel comfortable saying "No" to certain suggestions when they aren't in line on a resource or cost standpoint. It can be difficult to be able to say "No" because it can possibly cause someone to withdraw from the organization, however Sam takes it seriously and is open to discussions about what ideas can be carried out within the budget and timeframe of the club as well as the school.

Vertically or horizontally (with others and with leaders)

When you are establishing or running an organization, it's essential to receive the backing of your teachers. The support of teachers can develop the club as well as provide new opportunities thanks to the influence and reach of teachers.

Sam is required to frequently present his club's ideas in front of his teachers for the official blessing. It is essential for him to be comfortable in front of them and present his arguments with evidence to back it up. Furthermore, he needs to remain precise in communicating to the other members of the group.

Delegation

The club requires all of its members to take part for the achievement of its goals. It is not possible to accomplish this task solely by one individual or a select group of members. It would not only not be efficient, but it could contradict the goal of the group, that is to provide the opportunity for students to take charge of their lives.

Sam As leader must be aware of the strengths of each member and their preferences to assign appropriate the appropriate groups or assignments for each.

Relying on the experts

Within every club, there will always be an array of potential. The yearbook club is no exception. certain members may excel at photographing, while some are better with writing skills, and others are skilled at editing or creating.

Sam is required to listen to the experts in these areas and ensure that he engages the experts when making decisions been made on the subject. If Sam along with the other members of the club take choices in isolation this would result in an uninformed decision that would discredit the involvement of experts.

The expert's input assists in ensuring that all of the important information is taken into account prior to reaching a final conclusion.

Crediting others

The yearbook, as an example can be the result by a whole group, and it is not the product of one person. Sam and the leaders of clubs strive to invite members who assist with the tasks of the club. Not only does this make the individual feel appreciated and happy, it also helps create an environment of positive team spirit.

Sam will also highlight any exceptional effort made by fellow members each week in order to keep them motivated.

Owning your mistakes

Sam is, despite his age, is extremely well-behaved and has a high emotional ability.

It is not uncommon for school pressure to causes him to be less patient with other students. It's not often however, whenever it does occur, Sam catches it right immediately, identifies the issue, and takes care that stress is kept away from any interactions. In some cases, he meets one-on-one with the other person in order to say sorry for his incontinence.

Chapter 9: Leadership What It Is Not

It is a largely subject to interpretation. The definition of leadership varies based on the industry, culture as well as occupation.

Some types in "leadership" are nothing more than harmful and unfit for those who are subjected to the pain. Recent research conducted of DDI the Leadership Consulting firm, revealed that 57 percent of workers quit for lack of management. However, there are leaders who are more innovative that ensure motivation and morale remain the same and are generally raised.

After working in the technology sector for more than 15 years, I've seen many good leader and bad leaders. I have learned from both kinds. I've developed and adapted my approach to leadership in response to the experiences of these great leaders. Good leaders encouraged me to become a better leader, while the poor leaders helped me understand actions I needed to beware of.

In my professional life I've seen couple of different types of leadership that went wrong.

1. You can get things done regardless of "cost"

2. The leadership of leaders is fueled by fear

3. It is passive and never challenges the status that is

4. Expert in technical expertise, uninspiring leader

5. Never challenge or question executive's ideas

Let's take a look at each one of these categories more in depth.

You can get things done regardless of "cost"

Many leaders think their accomplishment is determined by the amount they ask their employees to perform. When they think about this often, they overlook all of the other aspects that need to be taken into consideration when managing an organization or project. It is important to maintain an environment that is positive for their team members, making room an appropriate work/life balance as well as fostering an environment that promotes team health by empowering their team members.

The results of this strategy result in the distrust and lack of respect for their leader.

Insecurity and fear fuel leadership

Through my own experience of both inside and outside from the office I observed that the majority of outwardly "bossy" people inevitably have an underlying fear of being seen as a threat. They use their bossy image in order to defend their own self-esteem; it's a defensive method of some sort. The leaders who are affected by this type of behavior tend to not accept new ideas. They often shutting down opinions from their peers and are prone to take it as personal if people don't agree with their opinions.

The combination of the factors mentioned above make the workplace a very unpleasant environment to work in. It is the reason why businesses lose many highly skilled employees.

It is passive and never challenges the status of the game.

It is a sour moment when I hear leaders declare, "That's the way we've always done it!" This is a sign which indicates that the leader isn't open to changing and doesn't feel willing to challenge an old-fashioned culture. When I hear the phrase, "Culture eats strategy for breakfast" and I can't imagine that a leader who is truly a good one can influence the change.

I've witnessed dramatic shifts in the culture of a company when a clearly defined plan is put in place by top management. If an executive can come up with an effective strategy to position an organization in terms of development and well-being There is always a chance to see a changes. The information can be communicated to different levels within the company. This strategy is now more of an obligation instead of an alternative. It's likely to create a large number of people feel uncomfortable, however this is what happens when you undergo changes in the organization.

People who sit in a secluded area and do nothing to address the obvious dysfunctions in the organization aren't able to claim to be as leaders. My opinion is that the best term to describe them is "Enablers" since they allow an unhealthy culture to spread its own culture.

Fantastic technical expert...weak lead

Have you seen the television show "The Office"? The principal actor, Michael Scott, plays the role of a successful salesman and manager. He is an incompetent leader who isn't able to earn admiration from the majority of his employees and doesn't have a clue about how to lead professionally his department. Even though Michael is fictionalized There is a certain amount of authenticity to how the portrayal of his character.

A person's ability to excel in their craft, it doesn't mean that they are able to lead; an instructor or mentor perhaps, but certainly not an actual leader. Many companies overlook this fact when they elevate the experts in their team to an executive position. The experts who are now leaders cannot make the right the right decisions, push others to think and support team members in difficult circumstances. It would be better off if they were as technical experts until they're trained as well as mentored, and equipped to lead.

Never Question/Challenge the Executives

They are completely aware of the strategies and directions of the organization. A company's success is dependent on strong leaders who are energized and aware of changing conditions in the market. They are not often able to be in tune with every day operations of the business. They are dependent on their directly reporting leaders and their direct reports who are on the ground to remain open about the risks and challenges they anticipate with the tasks being performed to support the company.

Managers who focus more to score points with management than painting a true impression are causing harm to their bosses department, teams and departments. The behavior shows an absence of moral courage and a lack of ability to be a good leader to the business in general. These leaders do not understand that executives trust them to be truthful and expect their executives to be honest with them whenever appropriate, instead of acting robotically "Yes, (Wo)Men" or "Brown Nosers".

Did you have experiences having "leaders" with the characteristics mentioned above? Perhaps, realizing that they false leaders can give the opportunity to renew your faith in your professional development and advancement as an individual leader.

The next chapter addresses the distinction between a leader as well as a manager. Both terms are often utilized interchangeably but there's a difference.

Chapter 10: Leaders Vs. Managers

In the beginning of my career, I thought of managers and leaders as a single entity. In the course of my career and became aware of the characteristics that distinguish someone who is a leader compared to one who is a manager. Everyone is a leader at some point, but there are a few managers who can be considered leader-like as is evident in the below diagram.

Managers vs. Leaders

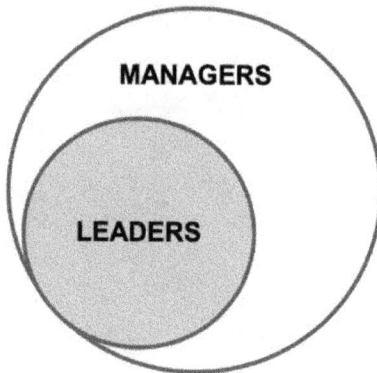

Leader

Here are some characteristics associated to a leader:

Motivates teams

Guides people

Creates new ideas by being willing to make mistakes

Credit where it's due

The work of a leader is more than just a job of executing.

Manager

The Manager however will have more particular responsibilities:

Make sure that day-today job is completed by time

Assists team members to set goals for their careers.

This allows their team to get the support they need to accomplish those objectives.

Assesses team's overall performance

Protects the team from "noise" i.e. distractions that don't need to be placed on the team.

The job of the manager is more process-focused and tactical.

Let's take a look at an example and see how it's handled by a manager and leader.

What is Leadership. Manage

AK Tech is a software development firm that is part of the Banking Industry. One of their groups, Team X is currently engaged in a major initiative to change the customer experience, and help create a company that is innovative in their field. Team X is a highly-performing team that is self-starters. The project has been mapped out and the team has been sat into the implementation stage.

As Team X is in the process of completing the project, a second request originates from an executive at the top of the chain. This is a strategy which puts the business on the same level as other businesses that operate in the same sector. It is a highly precise deadline, with financial consequences. However, the issue is that it demands an expertise that's exclusive to Team X.

Based on the fundamentals of Product and Project Management 101 It's obvious when Team X has to take the initiative in conjunction with their existing project it will need to be some fundamental re-planning:

Determine if your team is able to be able to take on this additional task without jeopardizing the existing efforts

Find out if there are other resources required to finish both of the projects

Examine the top priorities of every initiative in order to improve the team's efforts in alignment with the benefit provided to the client; delegate less important items

Create a realistic strategy that will meet the expectations of leaders

These are all the work of a supervisor. They manage and coordinate discussions with the other participants to put the process moving. An effective manager is organised as well as assertive. They also communicate efficiently. They are aware of who to rely on and the best way to delegate.

In the next scenario, suppose that, after planning, Team X determines that even if only the required components in place it is possible that the project will be completed a month after the time frame. As a response the C-Level executive reiterates there's absolutely no room for flexibility regarding the timeframe.

A typical "manager" would probably work with his team up to their limits to get their work accomplished because they believe their main responsibility is to ensure that everyone meet their obligations. Some cultures or even environments this could be viewed as positive or even cause managers appear "strong".

However, it is no good for management. This demoralizes employees.

A successful manager in contrast is able to become a leader within this context.

They could talk to the chief executive to understand "why" the new effort should be implemented immediately and gain a clear idea of the "value" of working on this initiative.

They must open with the executive team on the possibility of not being able realistically achieve the deadline with no significant changes in the work scope.

They may present alternative options for the executive to consider on the best way and time to perform the task and which other items may have to be moved due to the change.

The points above are actions which should be carried out by an effective leader. They don't hesitate to challenge decisions made by leaders and are more inclined to defend their employees. They always keep an "big picture" in mind and constantly think about ways to ensure lasting results and grow their employees.

Both Managers and Leaders are certainly important to an company, but both require different mental and working style. Like we have seen above the manager may take on the challenge and lead, however, it is not the case that all managers are leader-like or wish to be leaders in the real definition of the term.

Chapter 11: Interaction In Relation To The Authority

Are you caught in a position where you would like to have authority "authority" to direct a team of individuals to carry the idea you had in mind?

This kind of "power", if used appropriately, is useful in situations where you're the leader in the face of an emergency. However, it is important to remember that the "do as I say approach" does not build the confidence and trust you're hoping for over the long term. People are turned away due to the fact that they aren't sure if they're heard.

John R. P. French and Bertram H. Raven, social psychologists, conducted an experiment in 1959, which identified five different forms of power

1. Forceful Power - ability to force someone else to follow your instructions

2. Reward Power: Ability to provide rewards for doing something uninteresting to you, or remove rights if you fail to complete this task.

3. Legitimate Power - The power to make decisions based upon the organizational position

4. Referent Power - The ability to be influential by serving as an example of the standards that others may strive

5. Expert Power - Capability to be influential by being an expert on a particular subject

The initial three relate to a title or position that lets you make choices with consequences for those who don't follow or do not. The power of these types is much more to do with "authority", as defined through the title of the individual or position.

The final two forms of influence, referent as well as expert, are possessed by any individual regardless of their position at any position within the organization.

An Influential Case Study

Becky has recently been hired as a computer engineer by an Financial Institute. She has a wealth of experience and knowledge in this company based on her vast experience working in many different businesses and industries. Her team comprises five engineers, including a quality analyst, team leader as well as a product manager, and an administrator of resources. Resource managers are accountable for the team's goals and development of the team, while the team leader assists in conducting and overseeing the day-today tasks for the group. The product manager assists the team to learn about demands of customers. They also determine what priorities the team's efforts are focused.

After only a few months of working alongside the team, Becky noticed some basics inefficiencies among the group. The majority of time was spent reworking as well as deployments, which were much more manual. It was clear that the team was operating the same way for some time and was unable to address the issue because of the continual demands from them.Drawing on her experience in different companies, she realized that taking the time to tackle the issue will allow the team to take on additional work, without losing the quality. A few ideas she wanted to suggest included:

Automated testing wherever is feasible to reduce time and ensure the consistency

The Product Manager is now the customer's point of contact to manage their requests and provide that there is less interruption to the entire team

Preparing the team's tasks in shorter time frames and then resizing your deliveries in order to gain more immediate feedback and decrease work

As a software engineer she was not given any "authority" per se to put these plans into action. She was required to cooperate and interact with people who could assist in putting these ideas into action.

There's more to it than a simple narrative to convince her team as well as her supervisors to make these changes. So she created a list of metrics and illustrations of the benefits to be obtained.

The team leader was approached by her Team Lead to share her ideas and get their support to her thoughts. The Team Leader was receptive to her ideas, knowing that the improvements would not just the performance of the team and morale, but also their overall performance too. Together they came up with an idea to convey this information to leadership and discuss the advantages. Becky was aware that leaders might be reluctant to make a drastic shifts, and so she ensured that her plan offered options to address the changes with small steps. This also gave both the leaders and team members the chance to experience changes at the micro level and be comfortable with taking the next step in this direction.

Becky could put these improvements in motion within just a few minutes. The most important strategies that helped her accomplish the job were:

1. Formulate the idea and use information and images to help support your idea.

2. Contact potential allies. Allies could be those with the power to assist to gather the appropriate group of people.

3. It should be about experimenting - It is easier for people to experiment with small changes before making a decision to change the old routine. Changes of this magnitude can be intimidating.

Many of us underestimate our capacity to make a difference, mainly due to the belief that we lack enough "power" to do so. Once we can overcome that myth, we will feel empowered to express our ideas and have a positive impact on our workplaces. The ability to communicate your concept and the possible benefits makes you an effective the leader!

Chapter 12: Rick Parks

Rick Parks - CEO, Society Insurance

Leadership Journey

Rick was a leader since high school. If something was required to get completed, everyone turned to Rick for leadership. He would often ask himself frequently would be "Do I add the most value in this role?" If it was "Yes", he took charge of the task.

The same pattern was repeated throughout college as well as in the business world. The way he approached things was not "What's in it for me?" Instead, it was "How can I help and add value to this organization?" And even in the business world, his motivation was more about discovering opportunities to improve an organization through his experience and expertise, rather than determined to climb the corporate ladder.

In times of uncertainty like during the Covid-19, Rick had an approach that provided an optimistic and hopeful outlook to the employees. It was Communication! Rick was determined to keep in touch with his staff and the leaders of his company.

He was focused on the issue of transparency:

The issues on the table

The possibilities for change

The uncertainty areas

Information available at the point in time

Rick says the 3 traits of a leader who is successful are:

1. The drive to do something positive and the desire to aid other people

2. Be humble and not thinking that you're superior to others

3. A curious mind knowing the ins and outs of your organization and its constantly changing and changing requirements

Chapter 13: D. Holly Lifke

D. Holly Lifke - Chief Human Resources Officer and Executive Vice President, The Boldt Company

Holly always felt a profound obligation to assist the people who needed help. Her the infectious enthusiasm and energy, caused people to look to her to help whenever they needed an effective leader. She attributes her capacity to remain calm during a emergency to her mom who was her teacher. Her mother taught her to be confident, self-sufficient as well as self-reliant and flexible. It helps her guide people without ambiguity in the most difficult of circumstances.

The most important aspect of her life was three elements namely, the process of learning, adjusting, and adjusting.

Leadership Journey

In the beginning of her career, as she worked at FDIC at the time, she was offered the chance to conduct exams and also give classes. It was then that she realized why she was drawn to teaching. The reason was that it involved helping people:

Problem Solving

Connecting the dots

Helping them see what capabilities they were lacking

The process of laying out a roadmap that will allow people to realize their potential to the maximum

The willingness of her to put on her hat and work hard earned her the opportunity to test her self and develop as an individual leader. Her reflections on her experiences through the years like this:

The concept of leadership is one of obligation and honor - it does not revolve around egos or self-gratification. This is about servant leadership.

Faith has provided her the courage and ability to face difficult circumstances assist people in difficult moments, and provide them with faith and optimism towards the future.

It is important to identify your personality and what you'd like to do if you feel uneasy, then is able to make big changes. The excitement of change is that it offers the opportunity to gain knowledge and tackle the new issues.

The leadership style of a leader is crucial. The key is being open and honest, expressing ideas and collaborating. Leaders should be able to take ideas from other people and also be open to accepting that ideas of others may make a difference.

There's a lot to share. Concentrate on expanding the pie instead of dividing the pie. Create something bigger.

Humility is an essential characteristic. It is the ability to admit "I have a problem... I'm not sure... know...Teach me!" Leadership is not necessarily about having the perfect answer.

The hiring of a leader can affect the work environment in the manner they're trained to operate within a workplace filled with talented individuals.

The process of building trust and energy in teams instead of limiting imagination helps create a healthy environment where employees can develop and become more creative.

"Culture eats strategy for breakfast"

Holly believes in the importance of culture to be "How" you execute your strategy. Both must align.

Her advice is that a cultural system with a poor strategy may still produce some results, but the outcomes may not be ideal. If a bad culture is paired with a sound strategy contrary to what she says it will lead to a failing.

The term "culture" is frequently used to provide reason to not follow through an action plan or take difficult choices simply due to the fact that it goes against the established. The behavior must be rectified for the company to achieve success.

Affairing with the effects of social unrest and an Pandemic

As a response to recent tensions in the social sphere, Holly notes that we are all able to be influential even if we don't consider ourselves to be the definition of a "Leader" by title. It is crucial to acknowledge that we're each of us flawed. The need is to speak one another out, and also have the confidence to change our culture in a diversity and inclusive viewpoints by engaging in open discussions about these issues. The most important thing is to acknowledge every person's story, journey and beliefs.

Holly played an important role in the coordination of changes throughout the spread of the disease. Her main tasks were in the group that was focused on the well-being of her employees as well as the overall health of the company:

Communication. Keeping employees updated on developments and their impact on the organization.

Employee Safety - it involved regular communications with employees and monitoring of state-specific policies.

Work from home shifts that allow employees to choose based upon their comfort levels with regards to working from home or coming to work, as well as offering tools for being successful as well as supportive during difficult situations.

Supporting projects to meet the needs of customers.

This helped employees deal more effectively with changes, and helped them feel a sense of confidence in the management.

Chapter 14: Andy Weins

Andy Weins - CEO, Green up Solutions

The nature of leadership versus. Nurture.

Andy believes he is a natural leader. As a child, he was wildly rebellious and never strayed from his way. It was whether it was finding an initial job or leaving and doing what he liked He was the first person in his circle to take on these tasks.

He was a leader by asking questions. He often questioned the collective-think mentality. Experience in the military and its organization, gave him an understanding about "What right looked like". This influenced the way his approach to managing and leading.

Manager vs. Leader

Andy states, "You lead people. You control procedures." Andy provides the illustration of managing and leading at the warehouse. Managers control inventory and processes. Managers train, empower the staff, coach, and instruct to implement those procedures.

Andy says:

Leaders should be aware that the human mind is constantly changing.

Leaders help and inspire other leaders to foster an environment that allows everyone to figure ways to solve problems together.

The leaders don't just act based on the way that it's been practiced. They are the ones who challenge the established order.

Transitions within the Military

Prior to joining the military, Andy claims he was in the wrong of managing microscopically. It was a problem that remained during his time in the military, where he had the ability to influence compliance however he wasn't "leading". The wake-up call for him came after he was scolded by his squad's staff sergeant Sanchez who was in charge of.

Staff Sergeant Sanchez unflinchingly and honestly stated that he required greater autonomy, and was not getting it from Andy's leadership style. This provided Andy some food for thought. This was the moment when he decided to modify his attitude towards the employees who he supervised, paying greater attentive to the needs of his followers from him, and reacting with greater empathy and patience. It resulted in them getting more interested in his personality and also accepting him as an effective leader.

Challenges

"You can have a perfect process and perfect system, but if no one follows it, it doesn't really matter!" He says referring to a situation which occurred in Cuba.

In Cuba, Andy saw a number of actions that were unprofessional and morally wrong. The way he reacted to his superiors during the situation were not well appreciated and eventually led to his dismissal from the job. It was a tough time both professionally and personally. Sergeant Sanchez was later his mentor, was able to help Andy realize that even though his reasoning was correct in calling the things that weren't morally right, he had to take a different route in order to have his viewpoint accepted. When looking back, Andy learned that he required to alter his approach to make sure that it was meaningful to these superiors. That is, what did it mean to their organization and how can it help their business. This is more powerful as opposed to a pure emotional statement or the need to protest.

He summarises the experience this manner:

"Often the squeaky wheel gets the grease, but in this case, it got replaced, because it was affecting overall performance."

Entrepreneur

Andy's leadership experience has also extended into Entrepreneurship. The company he runs, Green Up Solutions, uses ultraviolet light technology as well as an antimicrobial product to provide security of hospital quality as well as disinfection in everyday environments. It serves places such as daycares, senior living manufacturing and gyms, schools, as well as other gyms, schools, etc.

When Covid-19 was announced the CEO realized just how inexperienced the company was due to the magnitude to which the services needed were. In the beginning, he needed to lay off some employees due to the fact that all businesses were shut down for a long time. Then, when it was time to hire again the employees, he took more deliberate selections about who that he wanted to bring back. He viewed this as an opportunity for resetting his company's culture to include people who had the proper mindset and the work ethic to be supportive of his mission and goals.

Tips for Aspiring Leaders

Andy's mantra for young leader is "Do the f*ing thing!" Andy encourages his followers to go about it in on their own terms and focused on outcomes. This will help guide the way.

Organizations vs. Culture. Organisms

If you are thinking about culture in the workplace, Andy draws an analogy to an organism, as illustrated below.

Function Organism Organization

The growth and characteristics of an organism are determined by the body's nucleus, and DNA. Determined by the group's population and the cultural norms

It is the mainstay of movement. The cytoplasm houses all of the essential elements needed to help an organism operate efficiently. Strategy and processes assist organizations to achieve their goals and succeed

Guarding against harm. Cell membranes control what enters and exits out. It's the duty of all cells to combat the effects of toxicity. Human Resources, Managers, and their team members have to adopt the necessary actions in order to lessen the effects of employees who are toxic.

New employees have an possibility to influence the company's culture just like how a new part within an organism triggers an alteration or reaction within the organism. They will be bringing in the new standards. Being able to entertain their views on cultural issues helps them feel more valued than being controlled.

In the case of toxicity, the burden lies on the whole organism or company to eliminate of "toxic" object or behavior.

Chapter 15: Rashi Khosla

Rashi Khosla - CEO, MARS Solutions Group

Leadership Journey

Rashi believes that she is as an "accidental" entrepreneur. In the desire to have time with her family and spend more time with her family led her choose the entrepreneurial pathway, giving her the flexibility she didn't have at her previous job. Work-life balance and values for family was what inspired the company's culture and attracted many people to her business. The company was to achieve sustainable, sustainable and sustainable development.

Fears

The biggest worry for Rashi was having to take a break from her work to pursue her entrepreneurial dream full time. She conquered that fear by getting involved in the industry and letting her experiences as a leader direct her. She did not hesitate to contact her family members, mentors and others who were leadership. They helped her believe that she could not be unsuccessful. As a perpetual learner, she was able to dive deep into the complexities of her company.

"Fear can either get you or can drive you!" she states. As Rashi's home was not entirely dependent on her earnings, she was thinking, "Why not do it? !" She felt the greatest fear was that of putting herself on the market. Rashi experienced Imposter Syndrome many times during the course of her journey. She learned to identify it, and then reel it back so that she doesn't fall prey to it.

Challenges

The biggest hurdle she faced in the beginning of her venture was finding her first customer. Being a woman as well as someone with a varied background, she needed to put in more effort than other people to assert her power and feel as if she was a part of the team.

Her work be the voice of her. The drive she had eventually brought about her success, causing others to see her as a role model.

Achieving an Pandemic

Two of the areas Rashi concentrated on in Covid-19 included:

1. Employee engagement

2. Security of the employees

She deliberately displayed vulnerability through sharing what she does at home, in video chats, so that others would feel comfortable sharing their lives in the same way.

She collaborated together with HR to plan regular activities to maintain morale, and make sure that employees took time off. Also, she devised a strategy to establish weekly objectives for employees to help keep them engaged and rewarding employees for their accomplishments.

As it approached the time to bring workers back in the office it was decided by employees (their preference) and formulated by HR, ensuring that every employee's comfort levels and ease of use were taken into consideration. Rashi claims that the business worked so smoothly within the virtual environment that she didn't have any worries about employees taking their time to return to the workplace. She was confident in empowering them to take that decision them.

Volunteering to help the community

Rashi contributes to community members in many ways. Tech Coalition and Returnship are two of her newest ventures.

Tech Coalition is an effort to be led by local Milwaukee businesses to draw technology talent from all over the world to help make Milwaukee into a more tech Hub.

To help with this program the woman has assisted women in returning to work by training them, and placing the women before hiring managers. The project is referred to in the form of "MARS Returnship". MARS Returnship is a MARS Returnship program serves as an opportunity for women who want to resume their careers within the field of technology after a break in work. It provides in-job training as well as mentorship and a team-based strategy to enable women for a successful return to work. This program aims at ways to provide women of high caliber tech talent to companies that respect gender diversity and equality.

In addition, Rashi serves on the board of Ronald McDonald House of Changes and also part of the Committee for I.C. Stars and Neolink.

Chapter 16: Brenda Campbell

Brenda Campbell - CEO, Secure Futures

Leadership Journey

Brenda has a degree in Social Work and started by reviewing the child welfare programs. The job was a lot of red tape and bureaucracy. It was not uncommon for her to take a challenge and developed solutions, and then pitched ideas to management, however, most of the time she couldn't achieve any progress because of the hierarchy as well as the budgetary restrictions of the business. It was very disappointing to her and she believed that she couldn't contribute to the improvement of that organisation.

Brenda shared her frustration with a close friend she referred her to a person who was looking to establish an organization that would assist teens in developing financial literacy. She initially felt she didn't have any experience in finance education, she had not having any experience in fundraising, and she had not ever led an organization that was not a non-profit. It was unclear whether she could manage without this knowledge. However, she recognized that her forte is in the development of programs, and that was her skills required. Her background in programming was used to develop an organization from beginning, and then put in place a an organization structure that allowed the company to support over 85,000 adolescents in the course of 14 years.

Challenges

As she began her journey into the position of chief executive in SecureFutures, Brenda found herself being a victim of Imposter Syndrome. It was not uncommon for her to second guess her choices however, with time she discovered that her intuition was spot exactly. Her confidence increased and her perspective and advice has been sought out by leaders in business and non-profit organizations.

Brenda mentions that she knew what the cause of the organisation was as her family was financially well off and she was also the first generation college graduated. Brenda understood the way in which this educational experience would benefit kids since she could have benefited from the program in her teenage time. This mission was very in tune with her.

Serving the Clients

Milwaukee Public Schools (MPS) was the initial partner of SecureFutures. The beginning of the partnership as well as with a staff of two people, Brenda took on all roles within the company. She was in charge of hiring, training and directing volunteers. She also created a curriculum to recruit board members and collected the funds needed to fund the programs.

As this was her first time as a director, Brenda surrounded herself with experts to assist her through every aspect of leadership in nonprofits and fundraising. Through networking, she was able to connect with expert leaders and gain knowledge from the interactions.

Then, she had to face the issue of being the only female at the beginning of board meetings. She was forced to accept, however, she worked hard to create more diversity and a greater representation of the board. She identified people who represent the communities provided for, and later hired people who were the best fit for the company. The result was greater confidence and respect throughout both the company and across throughout the organization.

Brenda utilizes a research-based approach to program and curriculum development. She developed a system that offers regular feedback from students teachers and other volunteers. This, in conjunction with the behavioral outcomes, allows SecureFutures to constantly improve the program. It makes SecureFutures above other companies which focus on financial education.

Covid-19

In the wake of Covid-19 The SecureFutures group had move quickly into virtual learning. It was a relatively new area. Since schools were shut and programs were canceled, certain ones needed to be cancelled. First priority was to provide instructions, as well as in order to account for different styles of distance education, and to assist teachers when teaching in a virtual environment. SecureFutures is an unique Money Path program, an application-based system designed to assist students understand the connections between their college or career plans and their financial goals is a particularly valuable resource for those in the online learning setting.

Social Unrest

Brenda considers silence to be an indication of indifference and acceptance. She believes it is our responsibility to all stand up and speak out to confront discrimination. The current social environment has allowed SecureFutures to engage in discussions that are open and to show their gratitude to their staff and customers who are directly affected by inequity based on race. SecureFutures is a team of professionals. SecureFutures team is prepared to intensify their work to promote the issue of equity and financial participation.

Chapter 17: Bill Bunzel

Bill Bunzel - Vice President - Property and Liability Insurance, Society Insurance

Leadership Journey

Bill isn't sure if he's as a "natural leader". He credits his teachers for transforming him into his current leader.

As an administrator, he believed that he should be the most intelligent individual within the group. He began to see there was much to be gained by listening to and speaking. He was aware that those around him had solutions and he was able to trust them and be supportive of the people around him.

He admits to being an ineffective leader from the beginning. His approach was to boost individuals' performance by pointing on their shortcomings and failings.

After some time it became apparent that his method wasn't working. The results weren't what that he wanted and his employees weren't happy too. The result was that he had to change his method of working:

He began with the intention to provide positive reinforcement, and to assist people in building on their strengths.

He was able to increase trust and confidence in them so that they began to take on things by themselves, and that is the greatest reward for any leader.

He stretched them out to accomplish things.

Bill Like Rashi as well as Brenda frequently suffered from Imposter Syndrome due to the fact that he often was in situations in which he wasn't the most knowledgeable. One way to conquer that fear was to:

Be vulnerable and open to your weaknesses

Recognize the experience of those in the teams.

Challenges

Bill declares the one of his greatest issues was not seeing the whole overall picture. It was imperative to understand everything in the business instead of being focussed on one department. After he recognized the importance of taking a wider view He made the decision to provide employees with the chance to gain knowledge about different departments. The result was that they grew and contributing more than their designated department. This gave them more satisfaction in their work.

For Aspiring Leaders: Advice

Bill gives the following suggestions to aspiring leaders:

Learn more about different areas of your company Learn about the bigger image and connect across the entire organization. This can open up new the possibility of development.

Find guides and mentors who can guide your development. Coaching outside from your company or department can help you develop broad perspectives on what it takes to be a leader in the context of your situation.

Achieving the effects of a Pandemic

Communication became crucial as the disease spread. Bill posted weekly news announcements and messages to his employees. The focus was on guiding his staff on how to care for themselves and get help for the uneasy and challenging time.

The employees he supervises are "the most important asset in the company". If they are healthy He believes that they will provide the best service for customers. provide the highest level of service to clients.

Chapter 18: The Emotional Brain
Emotional Intelligence

1.1 The Emotional Brain

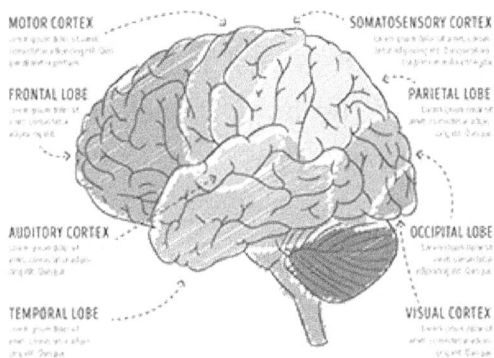

There has been an influx of studies about emotions, and the way that our brains perceive these emotions. The brain is among the most fascinating organs of the human body. the way it performs is intriguing.

Many studies and research has been carried out to discover the way that our brain operates and the various effects it has on our emotional state. The brain is comprised of various parts which work together to process data received.

From the numerous areas of the brain the limbic system is largest in processing emotion.

To gain better insight into the brain's emotional part It is vital that we know the many areas of the brain as well as the way they affect our emotions.

1.2 - The Limbic System

The limbic system, also known as the "central" component of the brain responsible to process emotion. This is why it's called"the "emotional brain."

The term is referred to as a paleomammalian cortex, it's located in both sides of the thalamus just beneath the medial temporal lobe of the cerebrum, primarily within the midbrain.

Alongside emotions, the brain also helps with long-term memory behaviour, motivation, as well as the sense of smell. Your emotional state is located within the limbic system which aids in the creation of memories.

The interconnected areas and the structure that make up the structure of the limbic system play an active role in the process of learning, emotion as well as motivation, memory and emotion. In order for the limbic system to be functioning properly, it has to influence the autonomic nervous system as well as the endocrine system.

The limbic system is in intimate relationship with the basal ganglia that receives signals through the cortex. it relays outgoings to the brain stem centres.

Additionally, it is closely connected to the prefrontal cortex. It is connected to the satisfaction you get when solving a challenge.

The relationship helps to treat extreme emotional disorders by the prefrontal lobotomy procedure, which is the psychosurgery process.

The connection to the cerebral cortex connects it to emotions, drives and olfaction. It also helps with memory, autonomic control, as well as pathologically related to epilepsy, cognitive disorders and other.

The limbic brain is believed for its many roles, including influencing the emotions of people, time perception, memory and sensory processing, conscious as well as motor behaviour/actions as well as control of vegetative or autonomic emotions.

1.3 - Hippocampus

This is a crucial area of the brain which serves as the main memory central.

The hippocampus can be described as a pair with one located within one hemisphere and another is located in another area. Its form closely resembles the shape of the curvy shape of a seahorse.

The hippocampus is where the memories are created and stored elsewhere of the brain for longer-term storage. It is a key component in the ability of our brain to move around our surroundings and to determine spatial orientation.

The hippocampus was found having a major influence on the process of learning. It is involved in the creation of neurons that originate from adult stem cells, which is an event known as neurogenesis.

Neurogenesis is a key component of neuroplasticity. It has a major role to play in the process of learning.

1.4 - Amygdala

The amygdala, which is the largest section that is part of our limbic system. It is involved in a variety of cognitive processes, and is considered to be an to be an integral component that is part of our limbic system. It impacts memory through the semantic division of episodic-autobiographical mind.

With the help of EAM networks the amygdala has the ability to affect diverse emotional reactions. The amygdala is able to perceive the emotional importance of events. This is the brain's central region of the brain that is associated with anxiety, and is a part of the response of flight or fight. An intense sense of fear or apprehension is often experienced by those suffering from seizures within the temporal lobe.

It's a crucial part of the brain that plays a role in processing of attention. Attention is defined as the ability to concentrate on a specific stimulus without ignoring others. This leads to anxiety and allows one to respond to anxiety by taking actions.

When the cells fail to function properly, they result in lower emotional performance that can end up with a higher retention rate of mental disorders such as anxiety.

The amygdala is also an important function in our processing capabilities. It's essential to the evaluation of faces in general. The brain plays a role in the general assessment of faces.

In the many studies conducted regarding the amygdala is concluded that it is a good tool to determine the reliability of a person. In addition, it assists in the assessment of first impressions of the person's appearance.

Human brains are an extremely complex organ that generates new discoveries each day. There is always something new that needs to be discovered.

It is not possible to say with certainty that we've scratched the surface with regard to a complete understanding about the brain of humans. It is nevertheless positive to realize that we're making tiny yet steady steps towards an knowledge of the brain.

The brain plays a major influence on the emotions we feel. The way that our brains react to external or inner influences can trigger feelings.

It is normal to experience a certain way it feels when in certain situations such as relationships, moods, or. The emotion may last some time, however sometimes, it may last for a long time.

The emotions do not appear in a vacuum, rather, they are the coordination of a series of responses which could result from emotional, behavioral, or neuronal or verbal mechanisms.

The role of the brain in the emotions of our lives is evident. It influences our feelings by way of perception, stimulation, and influences the way we feel and react.

It is a sequence of happenings that seeks to identify the variables associated with cognition and emotions.

The process of observing cognitive appraisal. it provides an assessment of things and situations.

The physical symptoms that are observed are mostly related to the physiological aspects of emotional experiences.

Action tendencies. This is the part that motivates us and results in the preparation and direction of motor actions.

The way one expresses It could be voice or facial. It conveys an emotion and conveys the intent or the reaction to an action.

Being emotionally involved; it can be experienced directly once emotions have occurred.

1.5 - Introduction to Emotional Intelligence

Similar to every other term is rooted in its origins as to how it came into become. We must dig details about its past to grasp the importance of emotional intelligence.

It was a term coined by two researchers under the name of John Mayer and Peter Salovey. However, it was famous thanks to Dan Goleman after his book was published and was titled with the same title in the year 1996.

In the research paper that was conducted by Mayer and Salovey it said that it could prove that emotional intelligence was measurable.

The term "emotion intelligence" is "the ability to perceive and express emotion, assimilate emotion in thought, understand and reason with emotion, and regulate emotion in the self and others" (Mayer, Salovey, and Caruso, 2000, page. 396; refer to Mayer & Salovey, 1997).

1.6 - Daniel Goleman

He has been credited with popularizing the concept of emotional intelligence. Goleman is invited to a variety of colleges as well as professional associations and meetings for business to talk about issues related to emotional intelligence as well as its impact on leadership and the way we live our lives.

As a psychologist having worked for many years and expertise, he is capable of presenting on the cognitive science and brain.

David Goleman has authored many books, including Leadership The Power of Emotional Intelligence, and The Brain and Emotional Intelligence. In his works, he's attempted to provide a thorough description of the concept of emotional intelligence, and explored ways that people are able to apply it to their own lives in order to attain high-performance.

The year 1995 was the time he published his first book in 1995, Emotional Intelligence. The book attempts to show how human abilities like self-regulation, empathy, and self-awareness can add importance to cognitive capabilities throughout the course of our lives.

It involves areas such as performing well in a place of employment, proving efficient as a leader, maintaining excellent health, as well as creating significant connections. In addition, when children are taught the skills of social and emotional development and skills, they will succeed when they reach the age of them.

If this policy were to be adopted it would result in an impressive performance of individuals which will make our community a more positive place.

It is easy for people to manage their emotions, and develop solid and long-lasting friendships that enhance the way people live together.

Goleman's book about Emotional Intelligence was one of the most popular books listed in The New York Times bestseller list for nearly two years, selling more than 5,000,000 copies printed worldwide.

The book was translated into 30 different languages and was the top-selling book throughout Latin America, Europe, as well as Asia.

The book that he published at the time of his death in 1998 Working with Emotional Intelligence says that when you can practice emotional intelligence in workplaces, it can lead to high-performance.

Alongside having technical expertise and intelligence, people also require mental acuity. It is a requirement for all employees employed in companies.

According to him, companies who consider this have greater chance of success in achieving the expectations or goals.

The year 2002 was the time he penned a piece about Primal Leadershipand the power of emotional intelligence. It was published by Harvard Business School Press and co-authored with Annie McKee and Richard Boyatzis.

The aim is to highlight the importance of emotional intelligence when it comes to leadership. As an executive, you need to know the emotional aspects of your personality so that you can deliver successfully. The ability to control your emotional state will help in achieving more effective outcomes.

The subject that is emotional intelligence a topic which David Goleman really advocated for and championed across the globe. He has frequently spoken on the subject in numerous gatherings.

There are many who claim that the concept of emotional intelligence is now being recognized to people via Goleman. In the course of time research has increased, and scientists have discussed this topic, in their efforts to understand the concept of emotional intelligence and provide detailed explanations of its significance.

Due to his efforts in promoting the concept of the emotional intelligence of people, Gellerman has won numerous awards and honors to recognize his work to communicate the findings of psychology of behavior to the general populace.

1.7 - The Beginning of Emotional Intelligence

It is thought that the initial time for the word emotional intelligence came into use in 1964.

This was invented by Michael Beldoch. In the year 1966, B. Leuner, wrote about Emotional Intelligence as well as Emancipation and Emancipation, which was published in the journal of psychotherapy the practice of child psychology as well as child psychotherapy.

Howard Gardener wrote a book, Frames of Mind: The Theory of Multiple Intelligences, in the year 1966. Gardener tried to present a theory that conventional forms of intelligence, like IQ cannot explain in depth the nature of intelligence.

The idea of multi-intelligence. It was a combination of interpersonal and intrapersonal intelligence.

In 1985, the word emotional intelligence was mentioned in a dissertation for a doctoral degree entitled The Study of Emotion: The Development of Emotional Intelligence in the work of Wayne Payne. The concept of emotional quote EQ was first mentioned in 1987, in an article by Keith Beasley in the British Mensa magazine.

Stanley Greenspan established a model which tried to define and define emotional intelligence. This was 1989, and within the next year, John Mayer and Peter Salovey wrote a book about similar.

However, despite all earlier mentions of emotional Intelligence it became a fad following the publication of David Goleman's book Emotional Intelligence-Why it is important more than the IQ. T

The book has become a best-selling book and it has also created the phrase "emotional intelligence" popular. David Goleman has written more similar books on this subject, which have helped to promote the usage of the term.

Current tests used to assess emotional intelligence have yet to be replaced by IQ assessments as a reliable measurement of data. EI is being criticized for its leadership capabilities and business performance.

1.8 - The Five Components of Emotional Intelligence

In the book by David Goleman Working with Emotional Intelligence, published in 1998, he describes the five aspects in emotional intelligence. Each one of them of the five is essential to its advantages. The five elements are:

Self-awareness

Self-regulation

Empathy

Motivation

Social skill

Self-Awareness

It is the ability to comprehend and recognize the person's feelings, motives and moods and that of others, and to understand how the emotions impact on the other person.

According to Goleman, in order to attain a state of self-awareness that one should be able to assess their feelings and recognize the emotions they feel.

Certain traits can indicate that an individual has matured their emotional state like confidence, and the ability to admit the mistakes you make and to recognize what other people think of your character. The author also recommends that people with self-awareness possess a strong spirit of humour.

There are many benefits to self-awareness

It improves the likelihood that you can handle constructive criticism in a positive way and knowing that it's not intended to degrade you and is instead intended to help you improve.

It aids in understanding the strengths and weaknesses of an individual. Through this, one will be able improve the performance of their team. The same can be utilized by businesses and organizations in order to make sure that they run efficiently.

Self-awareness will boost confidence in an individual.

It is an excellent method to carry out real-life self-assessments.

Self-awareness can be improved by:

Examining the responses you receive from people who are by your conduct and feelings

Be aware of the feedback is received from coworkers, since it could aid you in understanding the way others view your behavior and help you identify unhelpful responses

Keep a journal in which you write down the circumstances which caused you to feel a variety of feelings like anger, as well as your attitude and behavior when you are in that situation (with this information that you are able to comprehend your emotions and thoughts which makes it much easier to master self-regulation)

Self-Regulation

Self-regulation helps one control and manage their emotions.it does not mean you suppress or deny your emotions, rather you wait until the perfect occasion arises so that you are able to communicate your feelings. David Goleman suggested that high consciousness is likely to be a result with a high level of self-regulation capabilities.

These are a few benefits of self-regulation

People who have developed the ability to self-regulate tend to be able to adapt quickly and respond to changing circumstances.

It assists in managing conflicts and dealing with difficult situations.

This helps the ability to think rationally when faced with situations.

A person who is self-regulated is able to quickly gain the trust and respect of colleagues.

The self-regulation process can be enhanced through:

1. Knowing the moment you commit a mistake and accepting responsibility for the actions you took (instead of blameing other people and blaming them, you should take responsibility for your actions by acknowledging that you're in the wrong; people appreciate you for it as well as be less guilty.)

2. Behaving in a manner that is appropriate for you when you're calm (this will ensure that the message that you transmit is effective when you're in that situation)

Empathy

It is the capacity to recognize and comprehend other people's emotions. It is crucial for emotional intelligence. This is in turn linked to the way you respond to facts you are given.

When you come across someone who seems unhappy, it is likely to take special care so that they know you can empathize with their concerns and that you will do whatever it takes in order to help them are feeling better.

These are the benefits of empathy:

1. It allows one to understand the feelings of another and comprehend the reasons behind why they act in a certain approach. The ability of a person to assist them improves as you have an increased chance of dealing with the situation.

2. Employees are impressed with you and the performance of your job improves.

3. It assists in providing constructive feedback.

4. Being empathetic is a sign that you're an individual who is compassionate.

One can develop empathy by:

Imagine yourself in someone's position and assuming that they are in the same position.

Learning to pay attention to employees and not interrupt them.

Use body language to show empathy, and also to tone down the volume of your voice in order to convey sincerity

Observing those close to you, and attempting to determine their moods and their emotions

Not forgetting other people's thoughts and feelings

The ability to evaluate and comprehend the situation prior to making a decision

Motivation

This refers to the desire to achieve a goal using plenty of zeal and determination.

Here are a few benefits of motivation

It improves self-confidence.

It can help overcome the setbacks.

It helps to reach your objectives.

This prevents people from being a procrastinator.

If an individual is driven, those who are around him will likely to follow suit.

Motivation can be increased by:

Setting goals

Being optimistic

You can reward yourself with certain benefits in the event that you meet the goals you set for yourself.

Social Skill

It refers to the capability to discover common ground to manage relationships and establish networks.

These are some advantages from having social skills

It helps in establishing a relationship with your employees, and gaining the respect and loyalty of employees.

The people you meet will be at ease with you and it will be simple to discuss ideas and questions.

It is simple to interact with people.

Performance in work will likely to increase.

The ability to improve social skills is enhanced through:

Work in tandem with your employees

Understanding the art of giving constructive criticism

Developing practical skills in communication to be able to talk with people in your immediate vicinity.

The ability to pay attention to the opinions of others and their emotions and then acting in accordance with them

A problem solver most often when conflicts arise and you have to try to figure out a solution that doesn't rely on either or the other.

1.9 - What Is Emotional Intelligence? Emotional Intelligence (EI) can be often referred to as Emotional Quotient (EQ),

Emotional Leadership (EL) also known as Emotional Intelligence Quotient.

It's the capacity of people to identify their own feelings and other people's emotions, distinguish emotions and categorize them according to as well as incorporate them into normal thought and conduct and manage emotions so that they adjust to changing circumstances and reach one's goals. It is a very simple concept one could describe it as the ability to control and recognize your emotions and other people's emotions.

The definition of emotional intelligence has since been changed and redefined to include four abilities that comprise recognizing, using as well as managing emotions. In the present, there are three recognized models of emotional intelligence.

1. Model of ability

2. Mixed model

3. Trait model

Ability Model

John Mayer and Salovey tried to understand emotional intelligence, despite the restriction of it being a novel form of data. When studies were conducted however, there were a variety of definitions that were given to emotional intelligence.

At some moment it used to be "the ability to integrate emotion to facilitate thought, perceive emotion, regulate emotions to promote personal growth, and to understand emotions." After further study, the definition was changed into "the capacity to reason about emotions, and of emotions, to enhance thinking it includes the ability to perceive emotions accurately, to access and generate emotions so as to assist thought, to understand emotions, and emotional knowledge and to reflectively regulate emotions so as to promote emotional and intellectual growth."

The ability model identifies essential sources of data that help in identifying and understanding the social world.

They suggest that different people possess distinct abilities in relation to the ability to take in emotional intelligence, as well as having the capacity to link emotional processing with greater levels of cognition.

It is believed that this power will manifest itself through specific adaptable behaviors. The model of abilities consists of four types of capabilities.

Manage emotions. This can be described as the ability to manage emotions in an individual and with the other. Someone with a high level of emotional intelligence is able to sense movements, be able to control their feelings and manage these emotions to reach their personal goals successfully.

Making use of emotions. This is the possibility of using emotions in order to facilitate various cognitive tasks, that can include problem-solving and thinking. People with emotional intelligence are able to use their mood swings to the extent that matches the task they have to complete.

"Understanding emotions" - this can be described as the ability to comprehend emotions and enjoy complex relationships built around emotions. If you are able to comprehend your feelings and emotions, you have an increased risk of possessing the capacity of being sensitive to minimal differences between emotions, and to comprehend and describe the way emotions change over time.

"Perceiving emotions" is the process of identifying and discern emotions from images and faces, as well as voices as well as artifacts. Also, it includes the ability to discern feelings. Being able to sense emotions can help an individual who has emotional intelligence to efficiently manage other delicate information.

The model has however it has been subject to criticism because of its failure to work within a work environment. It's most successful with people who have proven it to provide positive feedback.

The ability to model EI tests are generally more efficient than self-analysis tests.

Measurement

The most recent measure in the ability model developed by Peter Salovey and John Mayer is called the Mayer-Salovey and Caruso Emotional Intellig test (MSCEIT). It's by a series of emotionally-based problems to solve.

The test evaluates emotional intelligence as an aspect of data. It is also based by analyzing the ability of IQ tests. The test can assess the ability of a person based on four EI capabilities to provide you with a score that can be summed up based on an examination of all four branches.

The concept comes out of the belief that the emotional intelligence of a person has a connection to norms of society. The results of the MSCEIT indicate that the higher percent of results indicate huge differences between individuals' answers and those derived from the larger population.

The amount of overlap determined by the different response as well as answers from the 21 researchers.

The issue is that the MSCEIT test might not provide accurate answers.

In addition, the standard for consensus scores make it challenging to find questions that only a tiny portion of respondents could answer as the responses seem to be logical and emotional in the event that a larger percentage of the respondents agree with them.

This has led to cognitive abilities experts questioning whether true emotional intelligence which is what actually defines intelligence.

Different measures have been used to assess the level of emotional intelligence.

Japanese and Caucasian quick test of affect recognition - The individuals involved are trying to find the faces of Japanese and Caucasian individuals who exhibit seven different emotions that include joy, sadness and contempt. They also show surprise sad, fear, and anger. Changes from one emotion to the other could last approximately 0.2 seconds.

A diagnostic assessment of the accuracy of non-verbal communication - it's built on the idea that the adult version of facial expressions includes 24 photos that have the same amount of fearful, angry smiles, sad and happy facial expressions that are low or intense intensities that are regulated according to gender. Participants are asked to finding out which emotion, of four, can be seen when presented with a stimulus.

The levels of emotional awareness Scale- participants have to read 26 social scenarios and responding to their anticipated feelings as well as the length of time they have lower-intermediate emotional alertness.

Mixed Model

The concept was first introduced through Daniel Goleman. It defines emotional intelligence as a broad array of knowledge and abilities which drive exceptional leadership. The model consists of five primary elements.

1. Social skills - This is having the ability to talk, engage with others, and maintain relationships so that it is possible to cooperate. Human beings, in general, have a social nature and can coexist through active interaction with each the other.

2. Empathy is the ability to understand and understand the thoughts of others and take into account the feelings of others when making choices.

3. Self-awareness is the process of understanding your personal strengths, feelings and weaknesses, as well as your

values, objectives, and motivations and being aware of their effects on other people when you make choices that could have an impact on the outcome.

4. Self-regulation refers to the ability to control or reroute an individual's emotions with a manner which is accepted by society and allows for responses or inaction and adjust to changes in the environment.

5. Motivation refers to the capacity of an individual to commit to taking steps to meet their goals.

David Goleman combines a range of psychological skills as he develops emotional intelligence.

He says that emotional intelligence is a skill one must improve on and isn't a skill you are born with.

If you make the right and precise decision to build emotional competence You can swiftly achieve the highest efficiency.

According to Goleman that people were naturally born with general EI which becomes the most important aspect in studying the power of emotion.

The model has been criticized as well as opposition from other researchers who believe it to be pop psychology in research journal.

Measurement

Two ways can be used to evaluate the model that is mixed.

1. The Emotional Competency Inventory (ECI). The ECI was established in 1999. The most recent version of ECI it is the Emotional and Social Competency Inventory (ESCI) it was launched in 2007. Emotional and Social competence inventory, university edition (ESCI-U) is available as well. Boyatzis along with David Goleman developed tools that provide a measure of behavior for the emotional and social competencies.

2. The emotional intelligence appraisal it was developed in 2001. It could be interpreted to be a 360-degree evaluation or self-report.

Trait Model

The term "trait emotional intelligence" refers to "a constellation of emotional self-perceptions located at the lower levels of personality."

A more simple way you can describe it by what people perceive as well as an individual's ability to feel emotionally.

The focus is on individuals' behavior and capacities that are able to be analyzed via self-report. It is in contrast the concept of an ability model which utilizes actual capabilities, which are in opposition to measurements made by scientists.

It is primarily based on the personality structure. You can also think of it as self-sufficiency in the emotional sense.

The ability model can be overlooked by this model. the model of ability.

Measurement

There is a range of tests that self-report emotional intelligence. A few of them include; Swinburne University Emotional Intelligence test (SUIET) and EQ-I. and the Schutte EI model.

They provide a bare amount of emotional intelligence. They only a fraction of the abilities, capabilities or information. The EQ-I 2.0 is one of the more widely used and well-studied method of self-report measurement. At first it was known as BarOn EQI, and at the time of its launch, it was referred to as BarOn EQ-i.

In fact, it was the first test of emotional intelligence that was available. As time it has become more commonplace. the same were discovered and applied to get better results.

The conclusion is that the focus is to improve the current method. It's proven more accurate than self-reports in other ways. The EQ-1 2.0 is now available in various languages and is currently being utilized worldwide.

The TEIQue (Trait Emotional Intelligence Questionnaire) is a test that attempts to clarify emotional intelligence in relation to personality. It is a test which has 15 subscales that are categorized into four factors, which are control of emotions, self-control well-being and social sexiness.

The psychological properties of TEIQue was examined through a study conducted in those who spoke French. the scores were found to be valid.

Researchers have also concluded that it's not linked with nonverbal thinking. Two studies recently were conducted which showed the comparison of several EI tests that showed positive outcomes for TEIQue.

1.10 - Importance of Emotional Intelligence

Based on evaluations of previous years as well as case studies, we have concluded that having an IQ of high IQ and not being intelligent isn't a assurance that you'll make the grade in your the world of.

Achieving academic excellence but not having the capacity to communicate with people in a social manner will lead in poor performance in the workplace at work. It can also affect your the relationships of others, and can also negative effects on your overall health.

Below are some of the advantages that come from having a high level of emotional intelligence.

The emotional intelligence of people helps build stronger social connections

In nature, humans were created to interact with other people. To be able to live well among ourselves you must know how to talk with each with ease. A person with a high level of emotional intelligence will be able to establish good relationships with those around him or their.

They are able to discern emotions, and knows how to react when and recognize situations that require absolutely no action.

This could help improving performance in the workplace or in any setting that deals work with others towards a common objective.

It alters the way we see others

What we think of others determines our relationship to others. The people who possess high levels of emotional intelligence usually present the best picture of themselves with others.

The majority of them to have self-regulation and show empathy towards other people. This trait brings them attention and demonstrates their trustworthiness.

It is possible to be secure around these people and develop strong bonds with them.

The ability to express emotions boosts confidence

Self-liberation occurs by being conscious of your emotions and can regulate and control these emotions. It helps you gain control on your self-control and gives you confidence with your choices and your identity.

Your confidence grows when you begin to manage your emotions with confidence.

It leads to better intimacy relationships.

The ability to master emotional intelligence can help you build strong bonds between intimate and close friends. EI lets you get to know each other and know how they behave, and help you identify the emotions they display.

Then you can understand the reasons you behave in a certain manner and reach an understanding wherein you can not make judgments about their choices because you have an individual perspective. The understanding gained from this process can lead to the creation of bonds that are unbreakable and endure for a lifetime.

If each partner has good emotional intelligence, the bond will endure for a long time.

A person's emotional intelligence could lead to outstanding academic performance

The EI trait has been linked to, leading to excellent academic achievement. A person who has EI is able to manage their emotions efficiently. This can help with managing stress.

It is evident that the person will not suffer with depression. This means that emotions that hinder performance are not a problem that leads to great productivity. A person is no longer a victim of struggling with emotions, which leads to a boost in their earnings to achieve the best results.

It improves psychological wellbeing.

Being able to manage your own feelings and to understand emotions of other people helps to live an amazing and enjoyable life. The confidence level of your friends is increased and this results in a higher self-esteem. It reduces a person's sense of fear and enables you to feel confident. In doing this it is evident that you are more comfortable as you feel confident about you.

This allows a person to develop self-compassion.

The people who have a higher level of emotional intelligence often love their own self and are confident about what they're like. They are able to recognize their feelings and are able to handle them.

They are able to make good decision when faced by a problem. Additionally, they seem to appear as being rational, and they tend to offer sound and unbiased guidance. Self-love is a crucial aspect for one's health and well-being.

People who have self-compassion are more likely to perform better overall performances in various life areas.

Effective leadership is based on emotional intelligence. skills

Good leaders must possess an emotional intelligence that is high. The leader is expected to be able read the emotions of others and understand what to do and when to not behave, based on the specific situation.

It's equally important to determine what motivates those under your leadership in order to determine the best way to inspire them to getting outstanding performance. As an executive, you must be able to connect with group to be able to connect with them and to create strong connections which can last for the rest of your life.

The ability to gain trust from people is important as it helps you become an experienced leader who is believed by the people. A high level of emotional intelligence can influence your leadership capabilities and will make you a successful leader who people be able to trust and follow. Future leaders must acquire emotional intelligence so that they can be in the highest level of efficiency.

1.11 - Emotional Intelligence (EI) Versus Intelligence Quotient (IQ)

What Is IQ?

The first thing to pop into our minds when we hear the idea of IQ is the amount of intelligence that a person has.

You may have wished you could be recognized as having a higher intelligence, as it could show that you're one of the most intelligent people. There's a great deal of research and science that is used to determine the definition of intelligence quotient. Below are some definitions to explain IQ:

It is the sum of scores obtained from a series of tests intended to evaluate the intelligence of humans.

The intelligence measurement can be displayed numerically format.

*IQ is the measurement of a person's capacity to tackle problems and think.

Certain scientists think that the tests used to assess the standard of intelligence are too limited and do not provide the complete variety of information about a person's personal.

Howard Gardener states that data is not just a singular capability. Gardener claims that individuals are prone to having strong points in a variety of areas, leading to a high degree of intelligence.

Comparing EI and IQ 1. EI is a term used to describe emotional intelligence. It is often times known as EQ that means emotional quotient. the term IQ refers to Intelligence Quotient.

2. The term "emotional intelligence" (EI) is the capacity to recognize how to manage and control the emotions of oneself and other people. The the intelligence quotient (IQ) is the score derived from various test that are standardized and designed to assess the degree of intelligence.

3. "Emotional Intelligence" (EI) provides one with the capability to understand the, control, analyze control, express and manage the emotions of oneself in addition to evaluating other people's feelings and understanding how to utilize the emotions of others to help in understanding emotions and thinking. significance. In contrast, IQ, on the side, provides an individual with the ability to research to comprehend, understand and apply knowledge to improve skills. It also aids in filtering out irrelevant information.

4. If you are working in a workplace In a workplace, the ability to express emotions (EI) aids in leadership in teamwork, developing good relations with colleagues, taking on the initiative and fostering the ability to collaborate. Intelligence quantity (IQ)will assist in dealing with difficult situations and gives an ability to assess studies and develop strategies which provide an answer to your current scenario.

5. The people with an emotional intelligence (EI) will likely be great leaders, develop into team players who are collaborative as well as socialize with ease and are more likely to be successful in a team environment extremely. People with an Intelligence Quotient (IQ) are extremely gifted and adept at handling difficult jobs. They have the ability to think and are considered to be the most intelligent individuals. They are thought to have the capacity to excel at jobs that require ability.

6. The phrase emotional intelligence (EI) was first introduced to be in the year 1985. The

idea was conceived in the work of Wayne Payne through a doctoral thesis with the title A Study of Emotions: Enhancing Emotional Intelligence. However, the term was popularized by individuals during 1995 through the publication of David Goleman. The book was written by Goleman; emotional intelligence: why it could influence more than intelligence. The term intelligence quotient was invented around 1883, by Francis Galton, who wrote an essay on inquiries to Human Faculty and Its Development. It was initially used by an French psychologist named Alfred Binet, in 1905 for the purpose of evaluating school children in France.

7. There are a variety of tests that have been carried out in order to determine the difference between them. To measure emotion-related intelligence (EI) there is the Mayer-Salovey Caruso Test (it relies on the ability to come up with problems-solving activities for situations that result of emotional states) Daniel Goleman Model Score (it is based on the concept of the ability

to express emotions). In the case of measuring intelligence, we can use the Stanford-Binet tests; Wechsler; Woodcock-Johnson Tests of Cognitive Ability.

Chart of Comparison

EQ IQ

Stands for Emotional Quotient (aka emotional intelligence) Intelligence Quotient

The definition of Emotional Quotient (EQ) also known as emotional intelligence refers to the capacity to determine, analyze and manage the emotional state of oneself, others as well as of other groups. A quotient of intelligence (IQ) refers to a number calculated from one of a variety of standard tests that are designed to measure the level of intelligence.

Ability to identify, assess the impact of emotions, manage and control one's own emotions, as well as perceive and evaluate others' feelings; apply emotions to aid in thinking to understand the emotional significance. Able to understand, comprehend and apply knowledge to including logical reasoning, language comprehension, mathematical skills spatial and abstract thinking. Ability to filter out unnecessary data.

Finds leaders, team players, people who prefer to be on their own, people with social difficulties. Highly skilled or talented people, those who have mental health issues and/or particular need.

The origin of 1985 was Wayne Payne's doctoral dissertation "A Study of Emotion: Developing Emotional Intelligence" The most popular application was made in the 1995 book by Daniel Goleman "Emotional Intelligence - Why it can matter more than IQ" 1883, English statistician Francis Galton's study "Inquiries into Human Faculty and Its Development" The first application resulted from French researcher Alfred Binet's 1905 exam for assessing schoolchildren in France.

Popular Tests Mayer-Salovey - Caruso Test (emotion-based problem- task solving) Daniel Goleman model score (based on the emotional capabilities). Stanford-Binet test Wechsler; Woodcock- Johnson tests of cognitive abilities.

Can EQ or IQ Be Enhanced?

Emotional Intelligence (EI)

A few scientists' assertions suggest that emotional intelligence increased, particularly in the early years. It is believed that awareness of emotions could develop at an early stage.

This is done through promoting traits like showing respect for others as well as teaching children to contribute with others, encouraging them to consider others' perspectives, increasing the individual's awareness, and encouraging children how to collaborate and collaborate with others.

Certain games and games have been offered in an effort to increase mental acuity. Learning through social and emotional (SEL) classes are provided to kids that are not performing when it comes to social interactions.

There is an opportunity for adult learners. This does not indicate that children can be the sole ones to get trained to acquire emotional intelligence. Adults are able to increase your mental acuity by effective coaching.

Certain diseases, for instance the condition known as high functioning autism (HFA) often known as Asperger's are associated with low empathy, which is one of the signs. Certain studies have shown an increase in emotional intelligence (EI) could change into individuals suffering from HFA.

Intelligence Quotient (IQ)

As opposed to the concept of emotional intelligence, there's an extremely low chance of increasing the intelligence the quotient. Intelligence is generally an talent that one was born with. But, it is possible to make it reach the maximum level so that you will be able to improve your abilities and succeed rates.

This is possible through having healthy food choices that enhance your brain's capability to give you the best performance. using puzzles that increase one's ability to think. This can increase the capacity of one's mind, by creating actual thinking tasks that require the use of their brain to think of the correct solution. creating problem solving strategies which force you to think outside the box to find an efficient solution.

With the data above it is clear that our emotional intelligence could be improved and the ability to learn can be increased. All you have to do is to adhere to the following techniques to increase your efficiency.

If you have children, it's crucial to establish the foundation of your child with regards to their emotional well-being at an early age.

If you do this by doing this, you can raise your child who is capable of tackling the challenges confront them in regard to their emotions. In addition you will be able to increase you IQ levels by challenging your mind with questions and solving the problems.

Chapter 19: How Emotional Intelligence Works

The use of emotional intelligence is across a variety of areas including in work environments as well as in business, and for building strong relations with other people.

It's all regarding how you interact with the emotions of others and with your own feelings. The term "emotional" can be used to explain how intelligence is a part of these ways.

2.1 - Emotional Intelligence in the Workplace

How can sensitive intelligence be important when you work? When you work in the workplace nobody tests the abilities of employees based on writing tests similar to those you had to take at high school or on campus to test your abilities or knowledge.

In this case, it's all about the way you present yourself and your image. How do you present your image when you are at work? Do you appear to be the type that is easy to trust?

Are we able to say you're trustworthy? Do you manage to connect with colleagues, or do you simply go to work, perform the tasks that are expected by you and are you are left to wait for another day? Here is where your emotional intelligence will come to the rescue. To respond to these inquiries accurately it is essential to be able to identify people with emotional intelligence.

To understand what happens to emotional intelligence at the workplace, it is possible to take into account the following elements:

Discipline

The majority of us judge people according to the character of their persona. What they do with others can tell us a lot about their character.

A person who is emotionally intelligent tends to be controlled. When you live your life, you'll be confronted with some irritants that make you test your level of discipline. Once you have mastered the emotions of yourself and of those around you, you'll have a greater chances of being able to react positively.

Know how to react with discipline when confronted in some provocative instances. Repress your emotions and behave in a manner that is appropriate.

When working in a set-up emotional intelligent people tend to be very productive since they've been taught to manage their feelings. There are a number of situations that demand focus in work.

If you are in a scenario where every one of the employees is given their own desks or workstations that they can work from If someone starts to form a habit of always leaving their belongings in your work area How would you respond to that? In the event that you had to react based on the way they feel, the odds will be that you'd react as if you were a twit and eventually show your frustration toward the person who is not yours.

But, if you're an intelligent and emotional person the response you would give is distinct. You'd practice self-control and deal with the situation using a great deal of discipline. Another option would include approaching the person in question and telling them it is not your style if you see them putting their things at your desk.

It will make them appreciate them since they are aware that you're able to handle your emotions with out involving others. If they're someone who is nice you can trust them to respect the space you have and will avoid placing items in areas that don't belong.

But at the time time it is important to be aware that humans have a tendency to be unpredictable. It is possible to approach them by way of greeting them and they may not show the same respect.

What happens if you let the other party aware of your feelings but they don't listen and believe that your views don't matter? What can a person who is disciplined and has an emotional ability, handle the scenario? If you're in a situation that's extreme it is possible to use a third-party.

When you are at work, it is possible that you may need to talk with someone who is in a more senior position. Tell them what you think about the situation, and set up a time scheduled for three of you to discuss the issue at hand. If you do this you have a good likelihood that you'll reach a consensus and resolve the problem.

It is likely you are able to gain respect from the people who surround you. That is because you opted not to be influenced by emotion, instead you chose to become an intelligent human being, and you acted in a manner that was rational.

Instead of being a bit obnoxious or creating a scene in which you let anger be the deciding factor instead, you decide to deal with your situation in a respectful manner, and then get the problem resolved. Whatever the fault of someone else has done, they'll respect the fact that you did not act in a way that they could have.

Self-Assessment

Sometimes it's essential to perform a self-evaluation. There are some companies that offer self-evaluation tests which they encourage their employees to complete. Personally, I believe self-assessment is more than the tests offered by employers.

If we were to ask you who you are, what response could you give us? Do you see your self? What are your thoughts about your identity? Knowing who you are is important at work. It helps you communicate with others successfully.

Spend your time to learn what you think about objects, your perception of the world around you as well as how you handle your feelings and the emotions of those around you.

It will let you shed the shadows of things you're not doing right as well as, at the same time it will show you the ways to do things correctly. When you are in the workplace Your actions and your tone influence how you communicate with colleagues, and will also impact your performance.

If you are taking self-assessment test You may discover that your logic isn't the same as other students. It is important to recognize that it's fine to have different views. There is no way to be 100% agreeing with everything because we see things in different ways.

If you follow this advice and following this, you'll feel certain of your opinions that will allow you the confidence to have a good time communicating your thoughts about certain topics. You will gain admiration because people will see confidence in your beliefs and recognize that their opinions are important more than other people's views.

They may not have positive comments. There will be some negative characteristics about yourself. This can be good or bad.

Being aware of some of these characteristics can give you an increased chance of improving these. There is a chance the qualities mentioned above can affect how you perform in your workplace, and that requires taking action to change. The person with the most emotional intelligence is able to control himself and performs well in the workplace.

Empathy

Empathy is commonly referred to as the ability to put yourself in the shoes of another. It lets you share the emotions of another person and comprehend why they act the way they behave. Being compassionate is not an ability that is available to everyone however, instead it is necessary to learn to behave with empathy.

The most emotionally intelligent individuals are more likely to have this characteristic which aids them to show their love for others. It is an essential characteristic to be able to display when working, because it can aid you to achieve a certain milestone.

Empathy lets you understand that the actions you take have the potential to influence the people around you in a direct way. It helps to gain the ability to control your emotions, and understanding how you feel can affect the atmosphere or mood of the environment around you.

Once you recognize the emotions that are in your head and realize the impact they can have on others around you then how you deal with the issue becomes a different one. At work emotional state is greatly, especially if you're the team's leader.

We will look at a boss or manager who isn't sure how to manage their moods and observe what effect this has on the employees who surround them. If you're at the top spot in your firm and you are constantly down. The next day you awake feeling angry over something that happened badly at home and your negative feelings carry onto the job.

If you're there when you are there, you realize that you speak up at any employee that makes a small error and you don't wish to hear what they've got to speak, so you place on them the pressure to succeed and deliver the outcomes you expect. Sometimes, you are able to fire some employees due to anger, which you do not hesitate to admit the decision.

What would be the reaction of employees under such circumstances? They're likely to be working to avoid angering you, and the fear of not performing, and the performance of their employees is predicted to fall lower than.

The person with the most emotional intelligence develops the ability to feel the emotions of those surrounding them and take care of the people around them. It is easier to be empathetic towards other people's feelings and learn to think that you are there, and this permits you to behave according to their needs. If this happens it is possible to understand how to manage your anger. It is no longer a problem to be sarcastic toward other people; instead, you let go of any issues, and instead deal with those you are leading well.

Learn to get to know your people personally and be aware of their feelings. Learn about their weaknesses and assist to make the most of their strengths. Being an effective leader in your workplace environment requires that the employees communicate in a way that they can comprehend.

If you show empathy you show empathy, people will respect them, which can increase their efficiency levels.

It is likely that meeting the goal is simpler because the employees feel at ease and motivated to achieve advancement. It is not just with employees, but also your clients. A few clients can be emotionally agitated and moody in specific situations. Others have a pleasant and professional attitude.

Sometimes, it is necessary to feel a part of their joy so that you know how to handle every one of them with respect that will be appreciated and be happy with your work.

Good Social Relations

Your interactions with individuals in your workplace is important greatly. This affects the kind of feedback you receive from those close to you. Each week, you spend much more time working with colleagues than with other people. It is vital to create a relationship with them and make them the ones you consider your friends.

Find out about who they are, what they like and dislike. Also and how they manage emotions, the things they are adamant about and how they view other people, and what drives them to improve their performance.

A person who is emotionally smart is able to hold conversations with everyone. What's more, it's not simply a conversation and it is valuable.

Recently, we've seen several companies who have teams-building holidays or taking time off from work. These are usually aimed at encouraging people to work in tandem in order to achieve great results. The idea is that when people are able to communicate to one another well and work well together, it will be simple.

Many of the top performing companies have managers who are able to connect with people. If you want to be a successful leader at work it is essential to communicate well with the people around you.

Make sure you take the time to get to know all employee thoroughly. It is important to do this regardless of the role the employer is in within a business. Make them feel that you care about them, and can relate to them in the same way that you do with those in higher positions. It will inspire employees to perform their job more efficiently and perform their work with enthusiasm as they'll know that they are appreciated by someone else.

Being emotionally intelligent will benefit employees. It's a skill everyone employed should strive towards having. This will help in the way you view your work. If you're satisfied with your colleagues, the workplace becomes an enjoyable and safe location.

It's no longer a matter of sadness since it's Monday however, you are looking eagerly to the next day to have an enjoyable week with your coworkers since they're the people that you've come to admire. Additionally, you can celebrate with each other and encourage the other when something unexpected comes out.

Motivation Motivation is crucial at work. It is the job is carried out for a substantial portion of the time You must feel motivated to do your best in working conditions that are effective.

A lot of people don't like their jobs or aren't happy with their jobs because they didn't choose to do it because they were looking forward to doing, or perhaps because of the atmosphere at work, or perhaps they work with unprofessional employers or don't feel that they're appreciated at the working environment.

Employers It is important to take care of the wellbeing that your workers enjoy. Find out what they think about their job. If you're emotionally intelligent then you can take advantage of their surroundings and put your self in their shoes.

If you find yourself in this situation it is important to ask yourself some key questions you must think about and then find an appropriate response. Are you content within the same setting? Are you in a location which can motivate anyone to put the majority of their lives within that setting? Are you able to wake up each day with a sense of excitement about the time you're going to your job? Do you work in a place you'd be happy to work at regardless of the position you hold? Do you show loyalty to your job, and you will never wish to look for another employer later in the future? If there were challenges that strike your work place Would you agree to work there until the conditions returned to normal?

By answering these questions and completing the above questionnaire, you will be better placed to understand how your employees feel about the workplace that you've created. If their responses are mostly negative, then it is time to change the workplace you offer.

It is important to show empathy and take into consideration the feelings of your employees in order to make improvements to feel at a level where feels appreciated. Workplace motivation directly impacts the work which employees give. For employers you must understand how to treat employees in a manner that makes them be motivated to bring about changes in their place where they work.

The motivation can be achieved through gifts that are given after meeting particular goals. In the event that you're a business firm, you may determine that any person who receives the number of customers you want is given a gift or reward in the form of things like gift certificates or furniture, devices such as monthly subscriptions, tickets for a show or to a concert.

It may seem little, however it will encourage them to be more productive in their job and will at the time at the time will result in a high level of productivity in the workplace.

It is also possible to set up contests between employers. It could be as simple as holding ceremonies wherein you award the top performers within specific areas.

There are categories that we can choose from including the most effective leader, the top accounting professional, the most successful marketer of the year, the funny coworker of the year, most efficient cleaner, the top team player, the top manager, the best put together, the cleanest behaving, the top performer of the year, and several more categories with the aim of giving recognition to the work of employees.

In addition there is the possibility of holding a teams building sessions where participants are taught to cooperate together. This should be a time for everyone employed in the business so that everyone feels equally valued for the effort they put into their work.

Furthermore, you can plan events that you have a celebration as a group. The event doesn't need to involve going to a class or do anything so make it a fun weekend filled with fun. It is also beneficial to create the surroundings suitable for work.

In the same way that you're continuously overwhelmed, attempting to plan your home's layout to make it comfortable just like you need to create your work environment.

Experienced designers are working on a great layout for your work environment. You must ensure that the workplace is the perfect environment for your employees. Ensure that the environment is a motivator for them to get up and go.

Being concerned about the wellbeing of employees can assist in making them feel more motivated. Women with kids that are still young You could create an area where the children are able to stay in and be looked after. Make sure that women and men have equal entitlement to pay based on their work hours. undertake.

Offer maternity leaves to pregnant women, and try to avoid working too much these women. Also, you can provide smaller meals for employees that they are able to eat during breaks.

It is possible to have a beverage as well as small meals that can be readily available to employees. It will let them know that you care about their well-being.

Employers as an employee, you can also inspire employees by offering them free days. Don't let them work too much with no time to take a break. Make sure you provide the quiet time at times when it's needed.

Additionally, you could provide medical insurance to your employees so they are well taken care of and they are not required to pay for hospital costs by themselves.

Additionally, you could provide an amount of benefits kind of allowances. For instance, the position could be accompanied by a house allowance, or an employee may be given the company vehicle, which could be used to carry out various tasks.

It is vital to be motivated in work. If you're interested in getting the best performance from your organization, it's important to let everyone feel respected.

The idea is to act as an entire family. This will at times, demand you to show kindness to others. If an employee celebrates an upcoming birthday, demonstrate your appreciation with a birthday party. event for them.

In some cases, disaster could occur in an employees' homes, requiring the intervention of an entire team to assist with the resolution of the problem.

A person who is emotionally well-informed will assist in creating a positive working environment that helps employees feel motivated and energized to work and do their best in their work. asked to complete.

These examples can assist in implementing a radical transformation in the work place.

2.2 - Emotional Intelligence in Businesses

It is possible that you have just started a enterprise, and now you're eagerly anticipating its success and hoping your results is great. Some companies can get difficult, and often, they require people have the stamina in order to reach the goals set.

www.ingramcontent.com/pod-product-compliance
Lightning Source LLC
Chambersburg PA
CBHW051727020426
42333CB00014B/1185

* 9 7 8 1 7 7 7 5 7 6 7 6 9 *